The Story of a Hurting Mom

From Broken to Mended

Cathy Taylor

The Story of a Hurting Mom *From Broken to Mended*

SECOND EDITION

Cover Design: Cathy Arkle – The Thumbprint group

For more information, please contact:
www.hurtingmomsmendinghearts.org
hmteam@hurtingmomsmendinghearts.org

Recommendations

Cathy is a leader's leader. She lives a life of compassion, vulnerability with truth. Her personal story will inspire you to become more authentic and open to talk about your own story. If you want to grow in your capacity to trust God with your difficult circumstances, read Cathy's story.

—Bob Newby, Celebrate Recovery Pastor-Southwest Church
Regional Director for the West-Celebrate Recovery

"You're not alone!" echoes from the pages of Cathy Taylor's amazing biography, The Story of a Hurting Mom: From Broken to Mended. *Her story is the human story, one of triumph and challenge, of setback and success, of pain and promise. As a pastor, advocate for women, wife and mother, my dear friend and colleague, Cathy Taylor, opens up her life like a modern day psalmist with an honesty and willingness that is more than courageous. The words on these pages reflect the redemptive power and love found in the One who shows compassion and care for us all, as we journey through life's challenges. It's a must read.*

—Marcus "Goodie" Goodloe, Ph.D., National Speaker
Author of KingMaker & HABITS

Cathy Taylor's story is a story rich in God's grace and healing. I have been able to witness first-hand how God has taken the hurting and broken pieces of her life and not only put them back together, but also to use them to help point others in the direction of their own restoration. This book will not only give you hope as well as moments of realizing that you are not alone in your hurting experiences, but Cathy also provides practical tools about the misbeliefs that often keep moms, and really most of us, from finding healing ourselves. Read this book to be encouraged, to know that you're not alone in your journey and to get pointed in the direction of healing.

—Mike Goldsworthy, Lead Pastor, Parkcrest Christian Church and author of "In God We Trust: When The Kingdom of God and Politics Collide"

The Story of a Hurting Mom by Cathy Taylor is powerful, insightful and can be pivotal for person who is caught between the joy of loving your child and the pain of disillusionment and fear that can make its way into the heart when a son or daughter is lost in their journey. I've known Cathy Taylor for over ten years and her tenacity and courage continue to inspire.

—Noemi Chavez, Pastor 7th Street Church in Long Beach, California, and a National Speaker

DEDICATION

This book is dedicated to my parents, Stan and Ruthie Brown, for whom and to whom I am so very grateful. They gave me unconditional love, even when I made choices that broke their hearts. They forgave me and showed me grace, even when I disappointed them. They continue to believe in me, affirm me, and pray unceasingly for me. Their lives exemplify the love, faithfulness, and servanthood of Jesus.

Table of Contents

INTRODUCTION

I'm not sure when being a Hurting Mom became my identity—the very essence of who I was—but for many years I woke up every day feeling anxious and fearful. I spent my days reeling with heartbreak and pain, and went to bed at night with a knot in my stomach that prevented any deep or restful sleep.

It seemed that most of the time I was simply "going through the motions" as I went to work, interacted with the rest of my family, and did the things that were necessary to exist. I felt as though I were carrying a weight that was so heavy I could barely put one foot in front of the other. It was difficult to smile or get involved in the banter around me and I had a hard time focusing on anything.

It all started when my daughter began to get into trouble at school in about the seventh or eighth grade. At first I didn't realize what was happening. I thought this was all normal pre-teen behavior. But as time went on it became apparent her rebellious behavior was more than normal teenage angst—something was very wrong. By the time she entered high school it was obvious that she had lost all respect for me. She didn't care what I said or did and she seemed to look for every opportunity to do the exact opposite of what I told her to do.

Some of the choices she made began to frighten me, and when I finally realized that she was using drugs, I started to panic. It was at that point I knew I wasn't dealing with the daughter I had always known. Her drastic mood swings, the cutting and hateful words she said to me, and finally, the way she would lash out at me physically, started to profoundly affect me. I felt as though every destructive choice she was making was deliberately aimed at hurting me.

I was much too ashamed to talk to anyone else about it and I felt as though I would explode with the pain and frustration of not being able to control my daughter. It was this situation that brought me to my knees. Out of sheer desperation and because I had nowhere else to go, I turned to God. I began to seek Him and would literally beg Him for peace and healing for my breaking heart.

As I read my Bible, I found myself clinging to the promises I found there—promises of hope and restoration, promises from a loving God who had created my daughter, loved her, and had a plan for her life. I learned how to surrender her to Him, and slowly I began to heal and to experience peace and even joy.

At some point during my process of healing I started to realize that my situation couldn't be unique. There must be other Hurting Moms out there who understood the heartbreak of having a child who was making damaging and destructive choices. There must be others who knew the deep inner pain, anxiety, and fear that I had experienced. A longing grew in me to meet with other moms who really understood my pain from their own experience so that we could share with each other in a safe place where there would be no judgement. I wanted us to be able to pray with one another—for ourselves and for our kids. I decided to find out for myself if all this was true—that I was not the only Hurting Mom.

I went to one of the pastors at my church and told him of my desire to start a group for Hurting Moms. I was given the green light, so I advertised in the church bulletin and told a few of my closest, most trusted friends. The first night, fourteen Hurting Moms showed up! This was the very first Hurting Moms Support Group. I really didn't have much of a plan so we just shared and cried and prayed and very quickly we began to experience freedom from our pain. What I now know that I didn't know then, is that talking about things—especially the painful things in our lives—takes the power out of them, and as we share, we move away from the bondage of our pain.

I went on to write the curriculum that we use today in Hurting Moms, Mending Hearts support groups at www.hurtingmomsmendinghearts.org.

In the pages of this book you will read about my personal life's story, as well as more about how Hurting Moms, Mending Hearts has evolved. I share valuable tools that I have learned on my journey as a Hurting Mom. I hope that as you read through these pages, you will be able to relate your own situation to my story and the stories of other moms that are told. It is my earnest prayer and deepest desire that the things I have learned and share with you here will help to facilitate healing in your life.

Chapter 1

Fond Memories

My earliest memories include knowing about God and Jesus. My dad was a minister in the United Methodist Church and I grew up in Sunday School learning about all the Bible stories and how to pray from the time I can remember. In fact, my parents have tape recordings of me praying at the age of three, "Jesus, gentle shepherd, hear me. Bless thy little lamb tonight. God, bless Mommy and Daddy . . ." and so on and so forth.

I was the oldest of three kids and our home was happy, loving, and safe. However, when you are a PK (Pastor's Kid) everyone knows your business. It's kind of like living in a fishbowl and everyone is watching you. From very early on in my life I was taught and expected to act in a way that would not embarrass my parents or the church. People knew who my dad was and who we were, even if we didn't know them. I was taught that appearances were very important and this would play out in some significant ways later in my life.

Ministers in the United Methodist Church get transferred around quite a bit. I was born in Chicago, Illinois, while my dad was still in seminary. He pastored several churches in the state of Illinois until he was transferred to Phoenix, Arizona, where we lived from the time I was seven until I was twelve. Then Dad was transferred to pastor Grace United Methodist Church in Long Beach, California. This was in 1963 and I was getting ready to enter seventh grade where I attended Jefferson Junior High School. I don't remember a lot about living in Illinois or Phoenix, for most of my vivid memories began in Long Beach.

Ministers don't make a lot of money, so going out to eat was a very rare occasion for us while I was growing up. There were a few times that we would have "grilled peanut butter" sandwiches for dinner because Mom was trying to stretch a very tight budget. It was always a treat to visit my grandparents who lived in another city, not too far away, because we got to have steak for dinner, which we never had at home. Those may have been lean times, but we always had everything we needed. We had new school clothes each year, and our family took vacations every summer. Our parents and grandparents always made sure that we had fabulous and often extravagant Christmases. What we didn't have, I never noticed.

When I was in grade school, we had a camper, the kind that sat in the bed of a pickup truck, and our family would go on camping vacations. When I got a little older, my folks bought a piece of property outside of Payson, Arizona, which they built on and added to over the years. When I was in junior high, Dad was able to get a whole month off every summer and he would drive our family over to the cabin at the beginning of the summer, stay for a couple of weeks and then return to California, leaving my mom, brother, sister, and me there for the rest of the summer. He would come back for a couple of weeks at the end of the summer and then we all drove back home together.

I have some great memories of my summers at the cabin, deep in the woods with the Upper East Verde River running right in front of it. We would have campfires, go on hikes in the woods, ride the neighbor's horses, play in the river, and fish for the trout that was stocked in the river each week. During monsoon season, in July and August, huge thunder storms passed through every afternoon and we would hunker down inside and read books or play games. It would clear off by dinner time and we would be back outside.

As I became a teenager, I was often surly because I was resentful at being away from my friends all summer, yet when I look back now, those were wonderful summers and they hold many of my fondest childhood memories. My mom told me years later that taking me there for the summer was my parent's strategy for getting me away from some of the questionable friends that I had chosen during my junior high and high school years.

Some of my favorite times with my own children were when we would take them to that same cabin in the summertime. I would show them all the things I remembered from my childhood. We would sing and roast marshmallows around a campfire, go for walks in the woods, and they learned how to fish for trout. My dad, their grandpa, taught them how to clean and fry the trout, enjoying many family fish fries together.

Today, my kids—now in their thirties and forties—love to reminisce about the cabin. Many of their best childhood memories are from those summers on the Upper East Verde River. We were all sad when my parents sold that cabin when they retired from ministry. As they got older, the upkeep became too hard for them so they cashed in all their assets to live in a retirement community in Prescott, Arizona. None of us kids were in a financial position to buy the cabin from them, so now another family is making memories in that special place. I have a beautiful oil painting of the cabin hanging in my living room and I often stand in front of it thinking about the good times we had there.

My mom did a lot of entertaining in our home and we often had guests for dinner. They were usually people from our church or other pastors in the area. We kids would eat at the table with the guests and our parents, so from an early age I was very comfortable in the presence of adults. It was easy for me to enter their conversations and I enjoyed being around them. One memory I have of those dinners with guests is the term "FHB". If our guests were unexpected, Mom would come around to each of us before we sat down to dinner and say, "FHB". That stood for Family Hold Back, meaning we couldn't ask for second helpings of food until we were sure our guests had had enough. We were always taught how to be sensitive to the needs of others.

My dad wasn't home very often as I was growing up. He was gone most evenings and of course as a pastor, he worked on the weekends. Dinner was always at 5:00 pm sharp because Dad usually had a meeting, or a hospital call, or a counseling appointment to go to after dinner. Most of Dad's time was spent outside of our home ministering to other people, his absence having a profound impact upon my life that I wouldn't fully realize until many years later. The question that one of us would ask every evening as we sat down to dinner was, "Dad, are you going to be home tonight?" It didn't happen very often, but we were so thrilled when he said that he was staying home.

He could never figure out why, when we were so excited to have him there, we retreated into our bedrooms or got involved in watching TV when he was home. It wasn't that we needed to have his attention, it was just nice to know he was in the house. We could hear his classical music playing in the living room or hear him and Mom laughing together. Everything felt complete when he was home in the evening.

The days that stand out the most to me in my childhood are the special days that I spent with my dad . . . just the two of us. Each year at Christmas I would receive a card from my dad with the promise of a special day. I remember everything about those days, where we went, what I wore, what we talked about. I remember vividly the time I wore a pretty red dress and my best black patent leather shoes. I must have been about seven or eight years old. Dad took me out to lunch and then to the library to get my first library card. The thing that

I remember most about that day, and we still laugh about it today, was when Dad blew his nose at the restaurant where we were having lunch. Now, when Dad blows his nose it is so loud and sounds like a trumpet or a bugle. I was absolutely mortified at the time and wanted to crawl right under the table, but today that is one of the fondest memories I have of a day with Dad. How funny the things we remember so clearly from our childhood memories!

I loved my dad and I never doubted his love for me or the rest of our family, but I never had the depth of relationship with him that I had with my mom. Dad and Mom had an amazing relationship. They had dated since high school, gotten married in college and had always been in love with each other. They had so many little private jokes and they could often be heard laughing together. They were always so affectionate with one another and in some ways we were always on the outside of something very special that they had between them. They made marriage look easy and I grew up thinking that once you got married that was what it looked like for everyone.

I was very involved in the school music program all through junior high and high school. I sang, played the piano, and I even led the children's choir at our church for a couple of years. I was the president of our church youth group. I was a member of a high school sorority. In school, however, I only got average grades. I walked home from school every day, did my homework and practiced the piano, which was a 30-minute per day requirement. I also babysat my younger sister a lot in those days. She was seven years younger than me and since my parents were often busy with church and community events, I would stay home with her.

All through my junior high years we lived in the church parsonage which was down the street from our church, Grace United Methodist Church. There were times when people in need would show up at our door for help or to seek counsel from my dad. One night when our parents were out and I was home alone with my brother and sister, a woman with three children knocked at the door. The children were barefoot and looked disheveled and cold. The woman was crying and seemed at her wits' end. Now we had been trained never to let strangers into our home without our parents being there. I talked to the woman for a moment and told her to walk down to the church and wait for my dad to get there.

My plan was to send him to the church to meet her when he got home. It was very cold that night and after waiting for a short amount of time I couldn't bear to think of those children and that distraught mom outside in the cold so I sent my younger brother down to the church to get them while I prepared something for them to eat. When my parents got home that evening they found the little family sitting in our living room bundled up in our blankets and drinking hot chocolate. It turned out that this mom had taken her children on the run from an abusive husband and, having nowhere to go, came to the home of the pastor in the neighborhood. I was glad that I brought them into our house. I felt like that was what I was supposed to do. I did not get into trouble for letting strangers into the house that night.

Another vivid memory I have from that house in Long Beach was the night our church burned down at the hands of an arsonist. In those days we didn't have cell phones, but we had several extension phones in our home and one of them was in my bedroom which was at the back of the house. It was in the middle of the night when the phone rang and woke me up. My parents must have picked it up right away because it only rang once or twice. I was just dozing back off to sleep when I realized there was a lot of commotion happening in our house. I got up and went into my parent's room where Dad was throwing on his clothes and Mom was looking out of the window that faced west, in the direction of the church. She pulled back the curtain and I could see that the sky was completely lit up with flames and hot embers were flying everywhere. I remember saying, "Is it the church?" to which my mom nodded her head.

I got dressed and my parents allowed me to walk down the street where I stood and watched as the sanctuary of our church burned to the ground. It was surreal seeing the firefighters do their work. I was overcome with emotion. I had never seen anything like this before and I couldn't get over the fact that this was our church being destroyed right before my eyes. There were flames reaching far up into the night sky and the sparks and embers were floating in every direction. In the morning ashes covered all the cars, porches, and lawns in our neighborhood. The next night another church in our neighborhood burned to the ground at the hands of the same arsonist who was arrested shortly thereafter.

When daylight came the morning after the fire, one by one the faithful members of our church arrived and we spent the day setting up our gymnasium, which was still standing in the unharmed education building of the church, for our worship services. We met in that makeshift sanctuary for several years until our new sanctuary was built.

Chapter 2

Commitments & Detours

I was fifteen years old when I accepted Jesus Christ as my personal Lord and Savior. I was at a summer camp up in the Sierras. One night the speaker invited anyone who wanted to start a relationship with Jesus to come forward. I found myself getting out of my chair and making my way down that aisle to the altar. There were so many young people that went forward that night the speaker asked for any parents in the congregation who had a child up at the altar to go lay their hands on their child while he prayed. I remember standing there facing the altar, waiting for what felt like an eternity, to feel the hands of my parents on my shoulders. When I finally felt them there with me, it was a powerful and very emotional experience. I had always known about Jesus, but this was my first encounter with having a real relationship with Him. Something changed in me that summer and I knew I felt different. I was more patient with my younger brother and I made conscious efforts to pray and read my Bible. For a number of years I grew in my faith. It wouldn't be long, however, before I found myself on quite a different path—a long detour away from Jesus—and it would be years before I made my way back and recommitted my life to Him.

Mom had drilled into me the importance of being a virgin until I got married from the time I first learned about sex. I was in fourth grade when Mom had "the talk" with me about that because I had been asking a lot of questions. She sat me down one evening when my dad was out of the house and my younger siblings had gone to bed and told me all about it. I was very close to my mom and we had lots of conversations about a lot of things. I can remember coming home from school, sitting down with her on her bed and talking about my day. I was always able to talk to mom about anything and everything. She was the central person in my life and since she was a stay-at-home-mom, she was always available. Mom was also the disciplinarian in our home. Dad always backed her up when she made a decision to punish one of us, but she was the one who we dealt with if we got into trouble. I never felt like she didn't have time for me and I never doubted her deep love for me. I received hugs and kisses every day and was often told how much I was loved. In fact, to this day she tells me how much she loves me every time I talk to her. I know how blessed I am to have her for my mom and I cherish the times we spend time together especially since we live in different states and I only see her a couple of times a year.

One of the reoccurring conversations Mom had with me when I was young was about "going away" to college. She shared with me about how important that experience had been for her and how it would also be important for me. I can remember as far back as elementary school, walking out the door and hearing my mom hollering after me, "Get good grades so you can get a scholarship and go to college." She knew that I would need a scholarship to be able to afford to go away from home to college.

I had a number of boyfriends throughout junior high and high school and I remained a virgin, mainly because I didn't want to disappoint my mom. In those days, instead of a class ring, the boys gave girls a Saint Christopher Medallion on a chain when they asked them to go steady. I was able to collect a number of those medallions during junior high and high school.

During my last two years of high school I had a boyfriend, Dave, whose dad was also a minister. Our families were very close and his family even had a summer home outside of Payson, Arizona, on the Upper East Verde River where we had our family's cabin. In fact, that is where our romance began. He was about six years older than I was and when my grades weren't good enough to get me into an "away" college, he and I got engaged during my senior year in high school. I figured this solved the problem. Getting married gave me an opportunity to be away from home in my own apartment with my husband while attending the community college in our city.

Dave and I got married the December after I graduated from high school. I was eighteen years old. Now when the minister's kid gets married, the entire church is invited and it was a huge church wedding with all the trimmings. There were months of planning, addressing invitations, trying on dresses and registering for gifts. Several women in the church put on bridal showers for me leading up to the wedding and we were married in front of five hundred people with both of our dads officiating the ceremony.

Dave and I set up housekeeping while I attended Long Beach City College and he went to work. He had already graduated from college and was a 'grownup'. I, on the other hand, was still a kid, hanging out with other kids at college and basically just "playing house" when I was home with Dave. I had been so caught up with wedding plans and dreaming about being a bride, that I had completely overlooked the fact that I had made a commitment to Dave, to love, honor and cherish him—for the rest of my life.

It surprised everyone when eleven months later I decided to leave Dave for another guy that I had met at college. The whole world seemed to collapse for my family. No one from either my mom or dad sides of the family had ever been divorced and I had just had that big, public church wedding less than a year before. Talk about shame and embarrassment! My parents were devastated and they basically shunned me in those first few months. I knew what I was doing was wrong and I was aware that my decision was hurting a whole lot of the people who loved me but, I was only nineteen years old and I allowed my heart to rule my head. Making life changing decisions by following my heart would soon become a pattern for me. It would be many years before I dealt with the intense guilt and shame that I carried about that part of my life. I never understood why, after growing up in a seemingly perfect Christian home, I made such horrible and damaging choices along the way. It was by working through the Twelve Steps and Eight Principals in Celebrate Recovery that I was finally able to understand that not having enough of my dad around as I was growing up had left an empty place inside that I continually tried to fill with men. It was in recovery that I discovered that Jesus was the only one who could fill that place that I had never been successful at filling before. And it was in recovery that I learned to forgive myself and move beyond my guilt and shame.

After I left Dave, I moved right in with my new man, whose name was Carl. I wasn't allowed to see my younger sister, or to show my face at our church. My parents didn't know what to do amid their pain and their shame so I was ostracized. I was nineteen years old and I had lost my family. Fortunately for me, I was so wrapped up in my new found love that I didn't notice too much at first. I was so self-absorbed. It would take years to unravel all the 'whys' of my behavior. As close as I'd been to my mom, I didn't see what all this was doing to her.

My mom had become a Hurting Mom. She was so full of shame and guilt that she didn't talk about it to anyone and began to isolate herself. It was hard for her to face the people at the church who had just witnessed my marriage vows and she had a difficult time supporting my dad in the ways she had always been able to do before. She told me many years later how she would sit in her living room quietly staring into space, <u>wondering where she had gone wrong</u>. She has also shared with me that it was during this time that her own faith in God grew stronger as she prayed for peace and prayed for me. In fact, she would pray for me for the next thirty years before I came back to the Lord and began to live my life for Him. In praying for my own kids today I often say to God, "Please, don't let it take as long with them as it did for me."

Seeing my mom in so much pain was breaking my dad's heart and he reached out to me several times. I remember finding notes on my car window affirming his love for me and reiterating that they just needed some time; that they hadn't given up on me. They were dealing with their own grief over my choices and I was so caught up in my relationship and playing house with Carl that I was okay with that. At least that is what I was telling myself. Deep inside I missed my family. I missed my mom, my confidant, the one who I had been able to share everything with all my life. I was working full time and taking a couple of classes at Long Beach City College, but the important things that were happening in my life could not be shared with her and it began to take a toll on me. I was still happy to be with Carl, but when I look back on that time, it was a lonely, sad, and empty time for me.

One day, several months into my new relationship, I received a phone call from my dad asking if he and my mom could come to our apartment that evening to talk with us. I agreed and Carl and I nervously awaited their arrival. He had never really met my parents and we had no idea what to expect.

They arrived with a bucket of fried chicken, asking for my forgiveness for shutting me out of their lives. They shared some of their hurt, but they also affirmed their love for me and told us that because I loved him and they loved me, they were willing to accept our relationship, and would like the opportunity to get to know Carl. They asked me to move back into their home and they even set up a roommate situation for Carl so that we could have a normal dating relationship instead of living together without being married.

Several months later Dad was transferred to a church in Tucson, Arizona, and a few months after they moved, Carl and I got married. We had asked one of my parent's minister friends to marry us. My parents knew we were getting married but we didn't want to put any pressure on them to come from Arizona to attend our very small wedding. When the day came, my parents showed up! They came to surprise us, ultimately showing us that we had their love and support. I didn't know it at the time, but this would be a pattern that was repeated two more times over the next twenty years due to my choices. No matter what I did or how hurtful my behavior was, my parents have always showed me the unconditional love and forgiveness of Christ. I am forever grateful that they never gave up on me. Little did I know that years later I would remember and draw strength from the example that they modeled for me. I had no idea that eventually I, too, would become a Hurting Mom.

Chapter 3

A Turn for the Worse

Carl and I were married for about five years during which we had two beautiful children. I stayed home with the kids for several years, but eventually went back to work. During our marriage I became restless and I cheated on Carl repeatedly with different men. It wasn't about love or even sex. It was about feeling desirable and wanted. Boy was I mixed up!

Of course my faith and commitment to follow Jesus had long been forgotten, even though we went to church on a regular basis. I was once again going through the motions without having a relationship with the Lord and certainly without seeking His direction in my life. Eventually, I met another man who I wanted to be with and history repeated itself. I left Carl and soon moved myself and my two very young children in with the new guy, Martin.

Martin had two small children the same ages as my kids

and after getting married we got full custody of his children. We started out our life together with four children, two five-year-olds, a four-year-old, and a three-year-old. Martin was Filipino so his kids were dark in complexion and hair color, while my two kids were blond with blue eyes. It was a beautiful family and I was fortunate enough to be a stay-at-home-mom for about ten years. We had a baby girl right away after we got married. Her name was Sarah and she was so special because she was related to everyone in our family. She was the one who tied us together, biologically. Eighteen months after Sarah was born we had another baby girl and we named her Leah. We were a full house with six growing kids.

Once again my parents embraced my new husband, as well as my step children. By this time they had been in Arizona for a few years so my actions didn't affect them as much because none of their church people or friends really knew me. They loved and supported us and although I know they must have been hurt when I repeated my pattern of leaving one man for another, they kept it to themselves and I never felt judged.

Martin coached all the boys' soccer and baseball teams and I was involved in the school PTA. The little girls were involved in Brownies and Girls Scouts and we attended the church in our neighborhood where I taught a Sunday School class. For quite a few years we were a happy and very visible family in our community. Those years of staying home with and raising six kids were some of the best of my life up to that point.

However, there were secrets in our house. For one thing,

Martin and I smoked pot pretty much every day. We would turn a fan facing out the back window in our bedroom and we would go in there, put a towel across the crack under the door, and smoke before every sporting event and family outing. We often laughed about how it made us better parents and gave us patience with all those kids. Another secret was that Martin was becoming an alcoholic. He worked in outside sales and would come home in the middle of the day for a few hours during which time he would drink several beers. I didn't get it at first. There had never been alcohol in my home growing up and I didn't like the taste, so I didn't drink. It didn't occur to me that this wasn't normal behavior and eventually Martin's alcoholism escalated and he started to become mean and abusive to the kids and to me.

This led to another secret. There were times when Martin didn't like the way the boys performed at a soccer practice he would bring them home and work them for hours in the backyard without giving them any dinner. I can remember standing in the bathroom window watching this with tears streaming down my face. I couldn't interfere or he would turn his anger on me and that always seemed to be worse for the kids. As time went on he became more and more unreasonable and he started to be physically abusive to me and the kids for no reason. I would watch him get out of the car at the end of his work day and try to determine his mood. If he looked angry, I would gather the children in the family room at the back of the house so they wouldn't get on his nerves. I felt like we were all walking on eggshells and I felt trapped with no way out. How would I ever be able to break up this family? How would I be able to support myself and the children? Leaving Martin didn't seem to be an option, so I stayed, covered up, and tried to make the best of it.

When our four oldest kids were in junior high school, Martin decided he wanted to buy a fish market and turn it into a "You Buy, We Fry" store. People could buy their fish and we would clean it and fry it up for them. I have never liked fish. I don't like the way they smell, the way they feel or the way they taste, but I went along with my husband, secretly thinking he was having a mid-life crisis. We borrowed money from family members to turn the simple fish market into what was basically a take-out restaurant. We installed fryers and fans and all the things required to fry and sell food ready-to-eat.

My husband was still working in outside sales, so he would buy and bring the fish and other supplies into the store and I was required to work there along with my sister-in-law to whom he paid less than minimum wage for working all day. I would clean the fish, sell it raw or fried, clean the fryers and everything else required for a such a business. My hands were covered with cracks and sores from handling the fish and I always had burns from the popping and sizzling hot oil that we used to fry the fish. I hated every minute of it, and the worst part was that Martin would bring our adolescent children in to work—in the afternoons, after school and on the weekends.

We needed help and couldn't afford to pay for it, so he had our kids doing the work. It broke my heart and I became very angry and bitter but I tried not to let the kids and especially my husband see it. I would go into the store early in the morning before I opened it for the day and would sit on the floor, rocking back and forth, crying and lamenting all by myself because I was so miserable and I had no one to talk to about it.

The store didn't do well and we were losing money every week. When Martin came into the store he would drink and become more and more angry and mean. I was very afraid of him by now but I kept quiet and did what I was told to do because I didn't want to get him wound up. However, watching my kids work like that, worrying about finances, trying to behave in a way that would not cause my husband to turn on me or the kids and spending my days in a fish market that I despised, began to take a toll on me and I started to shut down physically and emotionally.

We eventually let the fish market go because we couldn't afford to fund it any more. I got a job in the marketing department at a large construction company to help supplement our income. Although I enjoyed my job and I was so happy to be away from the fish store, thankful that my kids didn't have to work there any more, Martin's drinking was escalating and I was feeling more and more despondent about the situation in our home. I would dread coming home from work and especially the weekends because it meant I had to be around him. I was always grateful on the weekends that the four older kids went to stay at their other parent's houses because I didn't have to worry about protecting them from their dad.

Eventually, close to a nervous breakdown, I had to make the tough decision to get myself and the kids out of there. My parents had come to visit and we planned a family gathering; everyone was there. Martin was drunk and in his usual angry and threatening mood, and it was then my family recognized that something was terribly wrong. I had lost a lot of weight and I had a hollow and defeated look about me. I was quiet and withdrawn, which was totally out of my character. My family reached out to me and asked me if I needed help. Over the years they had witnessed other outbursts and signs of abuse from Martin and this time they decided to confront me with it.

The floodgates opened and I told them everything. I told them about my pain and my fear. I shared about how worried I was about our kids and how I felt trapped and didn't know what to do. They offered to help me financially when I was ready. I had been back to work for a couple of years, but I still didn't make enough to save a deposit and pay for the expense of moving out. For the first time I felt a glimmer of hope that maybe I could get myself and the kids out of the situation that was getting worse all the time.

When I began to make my plan to leave Martin, the four older kids were in their teens and the two youngest were nine and ten. One of the things that helped me to be strong enough to move forward with my plan to move out was that my youngest child, Leah, began to beg me to divorce her dad. She told me how she was afraid to come home after school if she saw his car parked in front of the house. I realized that this was not something kids in a normal family wished for and it motivated me to make some very hard decisions.

I knew Martin would never move out of the house we had owned for ten years together so I would have to be the one to leave. I spent several weeks cleaning out all the closets and cupboards and along the way I separated everything into two sections—the things I would take and the things I would leave for him. I didn't pack anything for fear that he would suspect what was happening. I planned, in my head, which furniture I would take and what I would leave. With the help of my sister, I found an apartment and my parents sent money to help me pay for the expense of moving. I can remember my sister literally holding me as I looked at places to live. I was so broken, sad, and defeated that I could barely put one foot in front of the other. I couldn't believe that I was breaking up my family and that soon my children would have to be separated.

Once everything was in place for me to leave, I talked to the older kids—one at a time—and told them what was happening. I told them that I couldn't afford to take them all with me, but that we would stay close and they could come stay with me and the little girls whenever they wanted to. I arranged for my two oldest to go to live with their dad, Carl, with whom I had remained friends over the years. I gave Martin's two boys the option of staying with their dad or going to live with their mom. She and I had formed a good relationship over the years as well. One of them decided to live with her and the other wanted to stay with his dad.

It is incredible how years of abuse of any kind can take their toll on us, often leading us to take dark paths. I'm sure it affected my children in ways that I might never know and certainly when I talked with them about my decision to leave Martin and move out, a relief came over them. I wish I had known what to do and how to help back then, but as a wife, I suffered consequences of this abusive marriage of my own and I just didn't know what was going on in the hearts and minds of each of my family members. We can become blind to the silent cries of those around us when we are in such pain ourselves. I did what I knew to do. I got out of this terrible, unhealthy situation and put some distance between myself and the pain.

As the day for us to move into our new apartment approached, Sarah and Leah were excited about our new adventure in our own home. To this day, they talk about the relief they felt because we were going to get away from their dad. Although they were relieved, I was reeling from pain due to the circumstances of the past few years which had culminated in this event. I knew that with time, I would begin to heal and I just wanted to get on with it.

On moving day I had arranged for our pastor from the church to come to be with me while I told Martin that I was moving out with the girls. The older kids went to school and the girls went to a neighbor's house, pretending to go to school. Just before Martin was to leave for work our pastor showed up and I told Martin what was happening. The pastor took him away just as a truck from my work showed up along with a friend bringing the moving boxes. Within an hour we had packed everything that I had set aside, moved out my part of the furniture, and were off to our new apartment a couple of miles away.

I'll never forget the despair I felt that first night in our new apartment. After living in my own house for over ten years, everything was now so unfamiliar. I could hear people walking around in the unit above ours and there were sirens and lots of traffic passing by on the busy street right outside of my new living room. Four of my kids had been dispersed to other homes in the city. I was alone, scared, and empty. I don't remember praying or relying on God during this time. In fact, although I probably would have said I had faith, I certainly wasn't seeking Him. I hadn't been to church or read my Bible for months and praying or listening to God had not been part of my life for a very long time.

It would be many years after our marriage had finally ended that I would hear about something called Post Traumatic Stress Disorder (PTSD) and it rang a bell with me. Maybe this was the reason for Martin's erratic and angry behavior. It could also have been the reason that he numbed himself with alcohol and drugs. While I was married to him, in the 1980's, no one talked about this disorder, but looking back, I believe this might have been what was going on with him. Martin had been drafted into the U.S. Army to fight in Viet Nam when he was only nineteen years old. He was injured twice while there and had scars and Purple Hearts to show for it. Recognizing this possibility gave me a different perspective and today, although I have no relationship with him whatsoever, I carry no animosity, anger, or bitterness towards him.

Chapter 4

Out of Control

I spent my first summer in the apartment lying out by the pool reading romance novels. I was healing and learning how to live without walking on eggshells. I was numb and emotionally unavailable to my daughters. Eventually I began to fill the emptiness by going out and drinking with the guys from the construction company where I worked. My girls were fending for themselves quite a bit and I was so busy trying to feel better myself that they were getting lost in the shuffle.

It was about seven months after we moved into the apartment that I met the apartment manager's son, Jeff. He was married with two kids and he was eight years younger than me. At first I just saw him around when he would visit his parents with his family, but then he and his wife separated and he moved in with his parents. He began to pursue me and it didn't take long before I realized that he was a full-blown alcoholic. That didn't stop me from falling in love with him and before long I was drinking every day with him. We moved in together within a few months and once again my pattern of jumping into a relationship repeated itself. I have often asked myself why I have always allowed my heart to rule over my head. Why, even though I knew intellectually that I was making a bad choice did I move forward choosing to pay the consequences later? It would be a number of years before I figured out the answer to that question.

Due to his alcoholism, Jeff had a hard time holding down a job and I was the main breadwinner in our family. I was always faithful in providing him with alcohol and I think that there was something about that which was appealing to me because it allowed me to be in control of our household. I don't remember ever wishing he would stop drinking, because the truth is that I began to drink with him every day. We lived together for six years without getting married and we were drunk every single day. I always made it to work, but there were many days that I worked with a serious hangover, only to make it home at the end of the day and start drinking all over again. Our life was chaotic, painful, full of turmoil, and totally without God.

Jeff had two young children who he was very devoted to and eventually he got full custody of them, even before we were married. Now that my oldest children were grown and out on their own, we had my two teenaged girls, Sarah and Leah, and his two elementary aged children, Sara and Nick, living with us. It was an interesting household with two daughters named Sara(h). We called my Sarah, "Big Sarah," because she was about six years older and quite a bit taller than Jeff's Sara, who we called, "Little Sara". Today we laugh because Big Sarah grew to be only five feet tall and Little Sara is five feet seven inches tall!

During the early years with Jeff I was so wrapped up in my relationship and in my addiction to alcohol that I severely neglected my children. My girls were basically on their own much of the time and they really didn't have much structure in their lives. They saw the ugliness of their mom being in a drunken stupor almost every day and they were exposed to the ridiculous arguing and fighting that was often the result of our drinking. I embarrassed them with my behavior and they eventually lost all respect for me, so that by the time I finally woke up and began to pay attention to them, my youngest daughter Leah, was out of control. This was when my journey as a Hurting Mom began.

One thing that I deeply regret when I look back on those years is that I didn't encourage Leah to develop her beautiful singing voice. She was in the vocal group in her junior high school and even got an award for being the singer with the most potential for advanced placement in the music program when she got to high school. I never helped her or gave her the support she needed to develop her voice and get more involved in music, which she still loves to this day. I often wonder how different her life would have been if she had gotten involved in music in high school.

In 1996, Jeff and I hit our rock bottom and stopped drinking. He attended AA meetings, but I just quit because he had quit. I didn't know anything about recovery or codependency at that time. However, I have learned a lot about it since and I know now that I should have been in recovery myself. If not for my alcoholism, then for my codependency and relationship issues. It would be a few more years before I walked through the doors of Celebrate Recovery and began my own journey of recovery.

When Jeff quit drinking in February of 1996, he went for a physical exam to see what, if any, damage had occurred due to his fifteen years of heavy drinking. He was physically healthy, but he was an emotional wreck and the doctor told him not to make any major decisions or changes in his life until he had least one year of sobriety. We waited for a year and a half before we got married on July 19, 1997, in Las Vegas. It was just the two of us. I guess you could say we eloped, although several people including our kids knew what we were doing. We spent the weekend there for our honeymoon and then went home to start our lives as a sober, married couple.

Chapter 5

Hurting Mom, Broken Heart

For the next few years my life was consumed with my daughter and her behavior. Leah was beginning to get in trouble at school and was becoming harder and harder to control. Even though I dropped her off at school every day, she would leave and her constant truancies eventually caused me to be ordered into parenting classes. I remember feeling like the scum of the earth in those classes. This wasn't the way I had been brought up and it certainly wasn't the way I had wanted things to go with my kids. I wanted to feel like I was better than the other parents there, but I wasn't. I was overlooking the fact that for the past six or seven years, during the critical times in her life, I had neglected her and this was part of the consequences. If I had to pinpoint the most important thing I learned during those weeks of parenting classes, I would say it was about the importance of families sitting down to the dinner table together.

When Jeff and I were drinking, I would usually cook

dinner, but I would leave it on the stove and everyone would just serve themselves whenever they wanted to eat and take their plate into their bedroom or eat in front of the TV. After the parenting classes, we implemented eating together every evening and some of the best family times we had during the years Sara and Nick were growing up were at the dinner table. By that time, Sarah and Leah were working in the evenings and almost out on their own, so they didn't have the benefit of those special times.

Many times Leah would leave in the middle of the night to go to her boyfriend's house and I remember literally getting into bed with her so she wouldn't leave. She would get physically violent with me and push me away and run out of the house. This happened on more than one occasion. My older daughter (Sarah) and I would often meet in the hallway in the night because we were both checking to see if Leah was in her bed. There were many nights when I found her bed empty and I would wake my husband and he and I would drive around with no idea where we were going, but looking for her.

She was eventually kicked completely out of high school for doing drugs on campus in the school restroom. She was sent to continuation school where she did fairly well until she turned eighteen when she dropped out of school altogether.

As I became aware of the fact that my daughter was using drugs, I began to be more terrified than ever. This was not the child that I knew and loved. The knowledge that she was using, which was causing a lot of her erratic behavior, paralyzed me with fear. Her own dad was pretty much out of the picture and Jeff was busy with his own two young children, although he was supportive and a great listener. We had talked about it when we first got married and blended our family and had decided that Jeff's role, especially since my kids were older, would be to love and support me as I parented them to the best of my ability. At the same time he would work to repair his own relationship with them which had been severely damaged during the years we were drinking. Regardless, I felt alone, anxious, fearful and hurt. I woke up every day with a knot in my stomach and sleep alluded me because I was constantly worried about her. It affected my job, my health, and the rest of my family.

I would stay home from work for days at a time trying to figure out what to do about my daughter. I think I really just wanted someone to fix her because I was quickly realizing that I couldn't do it. I checked into rehab facilities and found out that in the state of California parents cannot force their minor children into rehab if they don't want to go. Once, when I realized that she was driving the car that one of her boyfriends had given her with no insurance, no registration, and no driver's license, I looked into emancipating her. She was still a minor and I knew I would be held responsible if she were to get into an accident or hurt someone else. I found out that for her to be emancipated she had to be able to support herself, so that wasn't going to work either. Everywhere I turned I ran into a dead end and I was getting more desperate with each incident. She was destroying herself and I was allowing her to destroy me as well.

I remember once I called the police when she was smoking marijuana in her bedroom in total defiance of me. Two police cars came and while a couple of officers ransacked her bedroom looking for drugs, another big burly officer took her outside to talk to her. I could see them through the window and I saw him get about an inch from her face with a mean and scary look. But, she just stood there staring back at him with a smirk. It didn't seem to faze her in the least. When he finished talking to her she simply said, "F- you," and walked away. When that officer came back in the house he looked at me and said, "Good luck with that one." They told me that searching her bedroom was basically just for show and that they couldn't do anything about her. I think I really just wanted them to take her away so I could have a break.

One time she pulled a knife out of the waistband of her jeans and after threatening me she then acted as though she was going to hurt herself. This time when I called the police they evaluated her and took her away to a psych ward for a 72-hour hold. For the first time in many months I got a good night's sleep because I knew where she was and I was hopeful that we were going to get some help. That peace was short-lived because when we found out that our insurance wasn't going to cover it, they sent her home and we were right back where we had started.

One of the hardest decisions I ever made, ended up being one of the best decisions I made during those crazy years. Leah had a boyfriend who was abusive. I knew he was hurting her physically and one time after she had left him for a short period of time, he showed up at the house and she got ready to go with him again. I told her that if she got into his car she had to take all her stuff because she couldn't come back to our home. I helped her throw her clothes and belongings into trash bags and she left. She was seventeen years-old.

Leah was gone for over four months. I knew where she was and I sent her a letter letting her know that I loved her and she was welcome to come home, but only when she was completely done with her relationship. And then I prayed. Several things happened in the following months that convinced me that God heard my prayers and was watching over her. It was because of answered prayer regarding Leah that I slowly began to trust God enough to completely surrender her to Him.

The phone call came early one morning while I was at work. When I answered I heard Leah's voice for the first time in several months and she simply said, "I'm ready to come home." I immediately jumped in my car and went to the rundown, roach-infested building where she was staying, and she and I loaded her belongings into my car and I took her home. She never saw that guy again and I knew that as hard as it had been, the decision to make her leave was the right one. I had allowed her to pay the consequences for her own choice and for the first time she had had a taste of what that looked like because I got out of the way. She told me later that she had been miserable and it took coming to the end of herself and her pride to call me to bring her home.

Leah turned eighteen a few months later and things were calmer with her at home for a while. With her eighteenth birthday came a sense of peace for me because I knew she was now an adult and I wouldn't be financially or legally responsible for what she was doing any longer. It didn't take away the hurt or the worry about her, but it helped with my peace of mind.

It was the heartache and turmoil over my daughter that finally brought me back to the Lord. My life had been such a mess for so long and the emptiness that I had tried to fill with relationships, alcohol, and my kids was still there. I had traveled such a long road away from God that I didn't know how to pray or sense Him any longer. I was numb on the inside and my heart had become hard and stony. I didn't have much emotion at all and I couldn't cry and I rarely laughed. I knew I needed something to heal my heartbreak and to fill my emptiness so when my sister invited us to visit her church, Parkcrest Christian Church, Jeff and I went to try it out.

By this time Sarah and Leah had moved out of our home. Their lifestyle had become so different from ours that we were ready for them to go out on their own. When we would be going to bed at night they would be getting ready to go out, or vacuuming their room, or in the kitchen banging around. They were now nineteen and twenty and neither of them were attending college, but they were both working. We gave them a five-month window with a deadline to move out and although, they waited until the last week, they moved out into an apartment with each other and Sarah's boyfriend. That went well for a while and we enjoyed having peace in our home as we focused on each other and on Jeff's kids, Sara and Nick.

We continued to go to church at Parkcrest and that first year, 1998, I attended my first women's retreat with my sister and our mom. I vividly remember standing on the porch of our cabin with my mom and telling her how dead I felt on the inside. I told her how I wanted to experience the contentment that I saw radiating from the other women who were at the retreat. I wanted my heart to soften and I wanted to feel the emotions of joy and peace again. I couldn't get back in touch with that personal relationship with Jesus that I remembered from all those years before.

Chapter 6

A Beginning Restoration

Jeff and I continued to get more involved in our church. We joined a small group with four other couples where we studied the Bible and learned how to pray together. We got baptized together in 1999, and we began serving as greeters on Sunday mornings.

It was at another women's retreat a few years later that the theme Scripture verse was Ezekiel 36:26 where God promises, *"And I will give you a new heart with new and right desires, and I will put a new spirit in you. I will take out your stony heart of sin and give you a new obedient heart."*

When I heard that verse I remembered back to the first women's retreat and I realized that God had truly kept this promise to me. He had given me a new heart with new and right desires and I had emotions that I hadn't had before. I laughed and cried and my heart was not stony any longer. It had not happened overnight, but I realized then how faithful

God had been to me and I knew I wanted to spend the rest of my life serving Him.

God was beginning to become real to me again and I didn't realize it right away, but I was starting to feel the joy and peace that I had been longing for, although I was still a Hurting Mom. Within a short time after the girls moved out, Leah started dancing in a strip club. I didn't know about it at first, but I was devastated when I found out. I was shocked, hurt, frightened, embarrassed and very anxious and fearful for her safety and her soul. All those emotions were compounded when it became apparent that she was back to using drugs and her behavior became so erratic and even violent that Sarah and her boyfriend had to kick her out of their apartment. Even though she wasn't in my house any longer, that old familiar knot in the pit of my stomach began to show up again. But, this time I had a relationship with Jesus and I knew how to go to Him with my worries.

It was my faith that got me through the next three or four years. I learned how to pray for two things: the safety of my daughter and peace for myself. I also prayed constantly that God would protect her and bring people along her path that would be a good influence and guide her toward wanting to seek Him. God has taught me so much about His faithfulness over the years. There are many powerful stories of how He has shown up in my life as well as in Leah's life. In fact, as recently as a couple of years ago, something happened that reminded me again of how God answers our prayers and is always there, loving us, and arranging things behind the scenes that we cannot even imagine.

I met a wonderful Christian woman named Michelle. She was a Hurting Mom and had joined one of the local Hurting Moms groups I was leading. During one of the group sessions she mentioned that she was involved with a ministry that went into strip clubs on Friday nights and ministered to the dancers by giving gifts to them, talking with them, even helping them with their makeup and hair. I remember that Leah had mentioned to me that there was a group that periodically showed up in the club where she was working to basically just show love to the dancers. I asked Michelle if she had been to the club where Leah works and she said yes!

As we talked more we realized that Michelle had actually spoken with my daughter several times and she said that she always looked forward to seeing her when they went to that club. Since then, Leah has shared with me that she loves seeing Michelle at the club and the two of them have struck up a friendship. Never would I have been able to orchestrate something like that. Michelle going into that club is a direct answer to my prayer that God would put people in Leah's path who would guide her to Him. I like to believe that as Leah and Michelle spend time together, God is using Michelle to plant seeds that will eventually grow and develop into Leah having her own close relationship with Him.

I got to know a couple of other Hurting Moms at my church and when I realized how much better I felt knowing I wasn't alone and able to share some of what was happening with my daughter with other moms who knew firsthand about the hurt I was feeling, it had an incredible impact on me. It made such a difference and, somehow, gave me hope and relief from the constant churning I had inside.

Our church was very big on small group meetings and in 2001, the idea of starting a group for Hurting Moms began to take root in my heart. Surely there were others who suffered silently with nowhere to go and nobody with which to share my heartache. Maybe I could encourage other Hurting Moms with some of what I had learned during my years of suffering and pain. That is when I went to our small group pastor and told him about my idea. He was all for it and encouraged me to start the group as soon as possible.

For that first group meeting I really didn't have a plan or a curriculum. My idea was that we would share, pray, cry and support each other. What I didn't know was that sharing about our pain actually took the power out of it and we began to heal, just by talking in a safe place where no one was judging us.

Fourteen of us met for nine months and it was an amazing experience! We all shared our deepest pain with one another, each understanding what the others were going through. I recognized the power in that group, but I still felt it lacked a beginning and an end. I felt called to create something more that would lead Hurting Moms to a closer and more trusting relationship with Jesus, which was how I had experienced so much healing from my own pain.

As that first group wound down, I received a phone call

from our Senior Pastor one evening. He told me that he had been thinking and praying about a new position on the staff at the church and my name kept coming up. I'm pretty sure that my name was coming up because my brother-in-law was an elder at the church and he knew I had administrative experience and good people skills. My pastor asked if I would be willing to go to his office to meet with him so we could talk about it. I agreed and when I had my appointment with him he explained that the church was growing so rapidly there was a need for someone to organize and oversee all the volunteer ministries. It was a full-time position. He gave me a book to read and a couple of cassette tapes to listen to, then told me to think and pray about it, and to take my time before I gave him an answer.

I had been working in the construction industry for close to fifteen years by now and it was really all I knew. I never finished college and I didn't have a lot of confidence in myself, to say nothing about the fact that my life had been such a mess for so many years. Did my pastor and elder board members know that I was on my fourth marriage? Did they know I had been an alcoholic or that I still had a daughter that was out of control? Well, it turned out that they did know all about that stuff and they still wanted me to consider joining the church staff!

I listened to the tapes and read the book and prayed. It was scary to think of leaving what I already knew so well to start a whole new thing at the age of almost fifty, but I was intrigued and began to dream about what it would look like to work at the church. The deciding moment happened one evening while

I was out to dinner with my husband. We had ordered our food and as I was talking to him about this opportunity, sharing my thoughts and ideas, my heart was racing and my face was all lit up. I'll never forget when I finally took a breath from talking and looked across the table at my husband. He was looking right at me, listening intently, but he had already finished eating his dinner. His plate was completely empty and mine was there in front of me, untouched. I was so engrossed with talking about my ideas for the volunteers at Parkcrest that I hadn't even noticed my dinner had been served and my husband had been eating. I knew in that moment that this was what God was calling me to do. When I got home I called my pastor to tell him I was ready to take the next step.

After going through the application and interview process I was hired to join the staff at Parkcrest Christian Church, and in early June of 2002 I started working there. As of this writing, nearly fifteen years later, I am still on staff and grateful every day that God called me to serve him in full-time ministry.

Later in the summer of 2002, now on staff at the church and after I had led that initial group of fourteen Hurting Moms, I began to collect books on, "prodigal children." I pulled things from those books that were meaningful and helpful for me and came up with an eight-week curriculum. I studied Scripture to learn what God said about the different emotions we experience as Hurting Moms and I created fill-in-the-blank sheets. I put the curriculum in a three-ringed binder and used it to lead Hurting Moms groups for several more years. I was leading two groups a year at my church.

Leah continued to be a dancer and went through cycles of using drugs, drinking, partying and living what looked to me to be a wild and crazy life. She had relationships with several men along the way and I continued to rely on God as I learned to surrender her to Him. After all, God created her and loves her more than I do. It took time and practice but eventually the peace He gave me, when I asked for it, went from lasting only a moment or a few minutes to lasting for days and even weeks.

I can remember when Leah was younger and causing me pain I would say, "I can't wait until you have a daughter. I hope you get one exactly like you so you will know how this feels." Well, in 2003, Leah gave birth to a beautiful baby girl. Leah wasn't married, but the baby's daddy was there and continues to be part of my granddaughter's life today. I was in the delivery room when she was born and the moment I laid eyes on that beautiful child I took back those words. I determined right there and then that this baby girl would grow up knowing Jesus—if I had anything at all to say about it. And I would love her and be the best grandma I could be to her.

I have always felt that Leah's baby saved her life. As soon as she found out she was pregnant, she stopped using drugs and stopped drinking. She continued to work at the club as long as she could during her pregnancy and went back to it after the baby was born, but in so many ways she began to grow up. She now had someone else to take care of and be responsible for; a little person that needed her to be there. This was the turning point. Leah and I became closer than we had been in years and even today, almost fourteen years later, we share, for the most part, a close and loving relationship.

Of course, I still don't understand a lot of the choices that Leah makes and we still have our bumps along the way. We are two very different people, but that doesn't mean we don't love each other or can't have a relationship with one another. She has never gotten married and she still dances, but she is currently in cosmetology school and hoping to change careers when she finishes school. Her daughter is in junior high school and going through the usual adolescent attitudes, but she is a good girl and she and her mom have a lot of fun together.

A few years ago, Leah started coming to church. I was thrilled the day I got to baptize her. A couple of years later she and I baptized her daughter together —which will always be one of the highlights of my life. Her daughter—my granddaughter—is involved in the youth program at the church and it is my joy to see her there on the weekends and at other events.

Chapter 7

Stepping into Recovery

In 2004, the Celebrate Recovery ministry at our church was placed under my supervision and it was through this ministry that I began to recognize my passion for listening to, loving, and encouraging broken and hurting people, like I had once been.

My husband, Jeff, had already been part of the ministry for a couple of years, although I had never attended. When I got involved in Celebrate Recovery, as the staff oversight I acted as the administrator for the ministry, and I attended every Friday night, but I sat in the very back row and never went to small groups or got involved in a Step Study Group. I never got up front because at CR, when you speak in front of the group, you must identify your area of recovery and at the time I didn't realize that I needed recovery or had any recovery issues. I thought I was just there to oversee the ministry, train the leaders, take care of the scheduling and the details of the program.

The rest of the leadership team was very aware of my issues of control and codependency. I remember one guy saying, "When you bring the body long enough, the mind will eventually follow." Well, after an entire year of sitting in that back row and listening to the recovery teachings and the amazing testimonies of what God had done in people's lives, I finally understood that I needed to be there. I finally got out of that seat and began to participate in the small groups and got involved in a Step Study Group where I worked my way through the Twelve Steps and Eight Principles of Recovery.

It was through Celebrate Recovery that I learned to move completely away from the bondage of my past. My adultery issues and multiple marriages, my alcoholism and the way I had neglected my kids had all caused me to carry a lot of guilt and shame for many years. I had never understood what had made me do those horrible things. I had never talked about it or dealt with it and in CR, I began to peel back the layers and face head-on the things that were buried so deeply and were holding me back from being everything God wanted me to be.

I learned that because my dad was gone so much of the time when I was young, I had missed out on that kind of close relationship a dad daughter should have, one that I needed and longed for. It had left an empty place inside of me that I tried for years to fill with men and alcohol. I never knew what he was talking about when Dad had come to me years before asking for my forgiveness for not being there for me as I grew up. I now understood that just because he was such a wonderful man and minister and never abused or abandoned me, didn't mean he was a great dad. He did the best he could with what he had and today I appreciate him and his faithfulness to his family, especially to the Gospel. He and I have talked openly about the past and asked each other's forgiveness for our part in hurting one another. Just as I am in awe of how my dad has lived his life for the Lord so faithfully for so many years, he says that having lived long enough to see me come full circle and serving the Lord today is one of his greatest joys in life.

By working through the Twelve Steps and the Eight Principles of Celebrate Recovery, I went to a whole new level in my relationship with God, my family and others. It gave me new tools that I continue to use both in my own life and as I minister to others. Celebrate Recovery helped me to completely surrender my daughter as well as my other kids to God and to receive the peace that He so freely gives to us when we seek Him, even when my children are amid their own messes. I had no idea that being involved in and leading Celebrate Recovery would give me the tools I would need later when Hurting Moms again came to the forefront. I learned how to train and support leaders. I learned how to speak in front of people. I learned how to carry out the administrative duties of running a large ministry, and most importantly, I learned how to be obedient and to trust God to give me what I need to accomplish all the things He calls me to do.

It was a couple of years after I joined the staff at Parkcrest that my oldest daughter, Kristin, and her three young children came to live with Jeff and me. She had divorced her husband who had become a meth addict and was in prison and she had decided to go back to school to become a nurse. When she was about half way through nursing school she got deathly ill. She called me from the emergency room at the hospital to tell me that she was being admitted with a large kidney stone that the doctors were going to try to break up so she could pass it the next day.

About 5:00 am the next morning I got a phone call from the hospital telling me that during the night the kidney stone had lodged in a place that made her entire system back up and she had what they called septic shock. She had been taken to CCU because her kidneys had shut down and she was very sick. When I got to the hospital she was hooked up to all kinds of machines and within a few hours I was standing outside her room, watching through a window, as they intubated her because she couldn't maintain satisfactory oxygen levels. She was kept in a comatose state on a ventilator for nine days. It was touch and go at the beginning, and I learned later that there were a couple of times when they didn't know if she would make it through the night. She had what is known as Acute Respiratory Distress Syndrome (ARDS) and her lungs had ceased to function properly. Thankfully, I didn't do any research on ARDS while she was there because knowing more about how serious it was would have scared me to death!

For the next nine days, I sat in the corner of her hospital room. I tried a few times to go to my office to work, but I just couldn't concentrate on anything other than my daughter lying in that bed hooked up to all those machines. We didn't want her kids to know how sick she was and when they asked why they couldn't talk to their mom we told them the doctor just wanted her to sleep so she would get better. I would get them off to school in the morning before going to the hospital and then I would come home at dinner time to prepare a meal before heading back to the hospital. Jeff was so wonderful with them and he would take care of helping them with their homework, getting them bathed and ready for bed, and tucking them in at night. He was a rock and my true helpmate during this difficult time. I would tease Kristin later that I don't know if I was more worried about losing her or having to raise those three kids.

During that difficult time, God showed up over and over again through other people. I was so distraught and overcome with worry that it was hard for me to pray. But I deeply felt the prayers of my church family, my parent's church family, and many other people. I sensed God right there with me as I sat in that room and He brought people by, off and on, throughout the days to remind me that I wasn't alone. My friend from work came and made me leave long enough for her to buy me lunch; people from our church would come to visit and pray with me; the social worker at the hospital would come in every day and just sit with me quietly for a little while. I especially remember one very significant visitor.

Marilyn was a faithful member of our church and had been on our Women's Ministry Leadership team. A few years earlier at a women's retreat she had had a serious incident happen with her heart and for all practical purposes she had died. The doctors told her husband he should gather the family and make final arrangements for her because there really wasn't any hope. There were people all over the city, state, and country praying for Marilyn and she had a full and miraculous recovery. There was no other answer than that God had answered the prayers and spared her life. When she walked into my daughter's hospital room it didn't hit me right away, but after she left I realized that God had sent her to remind me of the miracles He performs every day. I was given hope for my daughter's recovery in that moment and I was overcome with gratitude for the way that God hears our prayers and is with us even in our darkest hours. I felt God's presence through Marilyn that day and I have never forgotten the impact it had on me.

Finally, after nine days, they allowed Kristin to wake up and were able to remove the ventilator. Even though she could barely talk because she had been intubated for so many days, she pointed to the corner where I had been stationed every day and she said, "You were sitting right there, weren't you?" She later told me that even though she was asleep she somehow always knew I was right there. It was a joyous occasion when we were able to bring her three children in to see her the next day. What a reunion that was!

Kristin had to start over again in nursing school and it would be a total of five years before she and her kids could get their own home and move out of our house. It was a long, hard five years, but I know that it was part of God's plan for our family and now that those three grandkids are almost all grown up, I look back on that time and am grateful that we could be there for them.

Once I got involved with Celebrate Recovery, I put the Hurting Moms program on my shelf for quite a few years. However, some other women at our church carried on with leading the group for a few more years. Ten years later, it was through my involvement as a Celebrate Recovery State Representative, that I was approached by an associate pastor from a huge mega church located nearby. We were meeting about Celebrate Recovery when the topic of support groups came up and I mentioned the Hurting Moms group, and the curriculum that had been sitting on my shelf now for some time. He asked if I would mind giving a copy of the material to his church so they could offer Hurting Moms groups. I was happy to share it with them, so I made a copy and took it to his assistant. They had led quite a few groups for several years when a publisher who attended their church saw it.

When I received the publisher's email, I thought it was some kind of a sales gimmick and I deleted it without answering her. A few days later she called me on the phone and asked if we could get together to talk. At first I told her no, I wasn't interested. Then she offered to treat me to lunch, so I thought, "What could it hurt? I'll at least get a free lunch out of it."

Little did I know she would be bringing reinforcements with her. She came with a couple of the leaders of the Hurting Moms groups from her church and they proceeded to tell me story after story of moms who had received healing and now had peace and joy because they had participated in a group. I was overwhelmed because I had no idea that this was happening. God was using that Hurting Moms material and I knew it had nothing to do with me! In fact, I am convinced that if I hadn't been obedient and moved forward with this ministry, He would have found someone else to do it.

I went home and began to pray about it and within a day or two I knew for sure that God was calling me to publish this material so that moms everywhere could benefit by going through it. It was just seven months later—thirteen years after I first wrote it—that the Hurting Moms, Mending Hearts Participant Guide and Leader Guide were published. Since then there have been groups springing up throughout the United States and Canada, as well as online.

I had no idea of the magnitude of Hurting Moms everywhere and I am committed to helping them, no matter where they are on their journey, to have peace and joy. I know from my own experience that there is hope and healing available through God and my greatest desire is for moms that are agonizing over their kids to find freedom from their pain and to develop and grow in a relationship with Jesus.

I am not only committed, but I am called to continue the Hurting Moms, Mending Hearts ministry and to equip and encourage moms to become Hurting Moms group leaders in their areas. The community of Hurting Moms is growing every day and my prayer is that the women who need to be part of it will find us and get involved.

Today, Jeff and I have twenty-one years of sobriety and we have been happily married for almost twenty years. Our kids are all grown with children of their own and we enjoy spending time with them and with our twelve grandchildren. One by one, over the years, our kids have begun to accept Christ and get involved in church. A couple of them are involved with their spouses in Celebrate Recovery. We continue to pray for God to touch the lives of the ones who do not have a personal relationship with Jesus yet, and we try to set an example of what it looks like to have a daily walk with our Savior. We trust Him in all things, including the salvation of our children and we have surrendered each one of them to Him, which gives us peace and freedom to love them where right they are in their lives.

God always has a plan and even if we can't see what lies ahead. I believe that whatever it is, He can and will use it for good. As I look back on my life, I can see even the things that have been the most painful and caused the most turmoil have been turned around and something positive has resulted. I am amazed that nearly every day God uses the hurtful and damaging decisions of my past to help me minister to others who are on the same path I was on. He is using the things He taught me through my experiences and pain over my daughter's choices to help other Hurting Moms find hope and healing. God is always working behind the scenes to reach us, and thankfully, He is working to reach our kids too. We can take comfort in knowing that He is in control and we can find relief in recognizing that we are not in control. The best part is that He is so good. God is good…all the time.

INTRODUCTION

MISBELIEFS OF HURTING MOMS

Along my journey as a Hurting Mom I have learned some things. I have learned that most of my fear and anxiety was caused by things that I believed to be true, but were, in actuality, not true at all. I have discovered that when parenting a child who is out of control there are four common misbeliefs—if we choose to believe them—that cause us deep and paralyzing pain.

A misbelief is something that we have somehow come to believe that is not true. Some synonyms for the word misbelief are *delusion, error, falsehood, misconception*, and *untruth*. Another word would be a lie.

Our misbeliefs are a big part of why we are Hurting Moms. They can be dangerous because they cause us to accept our pain and anxiety as our identity. We move away from identifying as a woman of God, a wife, a mother, a teacher—whatever other role we have in our lives—and we become consumed with and identify only with the pain of being a Hurting Mom. It's all we can think about and we begin to lose ourselves to an obsession with the child who is hurting us. Even though the misbeliefs are very real to us, we must get past them if we are to experience joy and peace in our lives again. The first thing we must do in order to move past the misbeliefs is identify them by giving a name to them.

Let me back up for a minute and talk about what it means to have a child that is "out of control". I'm talking about a child who is making choices and acting in a way that can ultimately lead to their own personal destruction and certainly can lead to damaging or even destroying our relationship with them or their relationship with the family. For some, it is drug or alcohol abuse, for others it is a child who has turned their back on their family and is living completely outside of the morals and values we have tried to teach them. Maybe you are experiencing anxiety, fear, anger, bitterness, resentment, or distraught over your child. If you are struggling with any of these negative emotions, it's pretty safe to say you are a Hurting Mom. And if you are a Hurting Mom, you most likely are a victim of misbeliefs.

I was a victim of misbeliefs. I understand your struggle. I identify with your pain. You might not have a support group such as Hurting Moms yet where you live, but you are reading my story now—and I can share what I have learned from these misbeliefs so you can come to a new understanding and actually change what you believe in a way that will help you move beyond the pain.

Chapter 8

Misbelief—I'm the Only One

When I was a Hurting Mom I didn't talk about what I was going through with anyone because I was ashamed and embarrassed. I felt isolated in that shame and carried my pain alone. When we quietly hold onto our pain, it threatens to bubble up and consume us. Somehow it seems easier, at least for a while, to ignore or stuff down the situation along with our emotions, hoping it will all just resolve itself or go away. We may suspect that there are other moms who are hurting over the choices and behavior of their children, but we really don't know the pain they are experiencing, just like they don't know our pain because none of us talk about it. We suffer in silence and we think we are the only one who struggles with what is going on in our life.

This is one of the misbeliefs with which we, as Hurting Moms, are burdened. We are sure that we must be the only one going through what we are going through. We hear our friends, co-workers, and other family members talking about their "perfect" kids and we hope that no one will ask us about ours. We want to slip through a crack in the floor when we hear people at an event we are attending start talking about their children. I remember how hard it was to hear about those whose kids were going off to college when my own daughter had dropped out of high school.

I vividly remember the sick feeling I had in the pit of my stomach as I listened to people bragging about how their kids were excelling at just about everything when my daughter was strung out on drugs and had just had her second abortion. It seemed like everyone except for me was living the fairytale life—the wonderful marriage with the white picket fence, and the children who could do no wrong.

Was I the only one who suffered in silence with a child who was breaking my heart? Was I the only mom getting up in the middle of the night to see if my child was still in her bed? Was I the only mom who had a child who didn't show up for school most of the time—even though I dropped her off every morning? Was I the only mom who went to bed every night with a feeling of dread about what the next day would hold and woke up every morning churning with anxiety and worry? I thought for sure I was. I think I felt that way because I was always comparing what I knew about my own child and situation to what I didn't really know about other people's kids or situations. All I could see was what was wrong with my family and what other families seemed to have that we didn't have.

But I was wrong. The thought that I was the only Hurting

Mom was a *misbelief*. The only reason I didn't know about all the other moms who were suffering was because I never talked about it and neither did they. We were all too ashamed to mention it because we were all afraid of being judged. No one and no place felt safe to share about our deepest pain.

It was my broken heart over my daughter that brought me back to church many years ago. However, just because I was ready to turn my life around and have a relationship with Jesus didn't mean that my daughter was going to embrace my new life with me. I was in such a fragile state that I thought that since God was changing me, everyone else in my family was going to be okay, too. Obviously, it doesn't work that way and I had a very long road of pain and heartache ahead of me. My willingness to change my own life was just the beginning.

Once I rededicated myself to Christ I began to seek His will for my life. And as God started to work in me and to heal me from my guilt and shame over what my life had been and how badly I had messed up with my kids, I slowly started to see myself the way He sees me. I began to accept the fact that I was no longer the person who had messed up so badly. I was brand new. I was a new person in Christ Jesus and I was loved and valued. God had created me for a reason. He had a plan in mind and I was excited to find out what that plan was and to move forward with a fresh start in my life.

Although I started to feel better about myself, I was still very brokenhearted over my daughter and I still didn't talk about it, especially with my new church friends. In fact, I spent time covering up what was really going on in my home with the people in our church because they all seemed to have everything together and I didn't want to be judged or looked down upon.

As I grew closer to the Lord, I was bombarded with an intense longing to be able to share my pain in a safe place. I didn't know where that safe place would be, so I began to pray and seek God's wisdom. I asked Him to lead me to a place where I could share without worrying about the guilt and shame that were always lurking around me. I asked Him to show me how I could find the healing I so desperately desired.

I woke up one morning with an idea, an idea that I know was God's answer to my prayer. He gave me the idea to start a support group for Hurting Moms. A group that would provide a safe place for Hurting Moms to share their pain. A group like the one to which I had been asking Him to lead me. Well, this wasn't the answer I had anticipated! I was thinking more in terms of a safe place where I could go to *meet* with other moms. A group that was already established and where someone else was the leader.

I argued with God about it for a couple of weeks, but He kept reminding me of my commitment to being obedient, so I finally surrendered and made an appointment with the pastor in charge of small groups at our church. By this time I had talked to couple of other moms in our church who I knew were struggling and the more the idea took shape in my head, the more I knew that this was what I was supposed to do.

Fourteen moms showed up to that first Hurting Moms Support group. We went around the room and shared our stories, cried, encouraged one another, and prayed for each other. We left that first group gathering with hope and healing in our hearts, simply because we had had an opportunity to share our stories and our pain. And as we shared and listened it became clear that none of us were alone. We were not the only one. I learned that night, because I was willing to become vulnerable and share first, it gave permission and courage to the other moms in the group to be vulnerable as well.

Another thing that happened as we shared our sorrow and pain over our children with each other is that we learned the importance of listening and being listened to with compassion and empathy. Nobody besides another Hurting Mom truly understands the dynamics and emotions that we experience when we are in this situation and it was a unique experience to hear and be heard by others just like us.

I will never forget the freedom I felt that night after sharing my deepest pain with other moms who totally understood where I was coming from. It was one of the most freeing experiences of my life and I learned that talking about things takes the power out of them. When we hold our sorrow and anxiety in and are afraid to tell anyone, it makes us sick inside. Our pain holds us hostage and prevents us from experiencing life in the way that God intends for us to experience it.

One of the most powerful things about being part of Hurting Moms Support Group is that we begin to understand that we are not alone. There are other moms that are suffering with the same pain because their kids are doing some of the same things that our kids are doing. We can support and encourage one another at a level that cannot be obtained in any other setting. I think of the Scripture verse in 1 Thessalonians 5:11 that says, "Therefore encourage one another and build each other up, just as in fact you are doing."

That's it! That's exactly what we do in a Hurting Moms Support Group. I don't think we are meant to suffer in silence. We will never experience the healing from our pain when we are alone and isolated that we can achieve when we are together in community. I love what my friend Regina says, "Hurting Moms, Mending Hearts helped me by allowing me to surround myself with other moms going through the same thing I'm going through. It gave me a sense of empowerment. It gave me a sisterhood. It gave me a place where I could be transparent."

I have a friend named Brenda who joined her first Hurting Moms group a number of years ago. She said that because I took the risk to be open with her about my struggles with my daughter that it paved the way and made her feel safe to share openly about her son. That's the thing that we don't realize when we are going through this alone. There are other moms in the same situation who are longing to be able to be real about what is going on in their lives with their children. It only takes one person who is willing to step out in faith to share their story for others to have the courage to do the same.

Several years after Brenda went through her first Hurting

Moms group she was co-leading another group and the very first night of the group, in walked a mom whom Brenda had known in high school but hadn't seen since, except for one time when they had run into each other in the grocery store. They both remembered it. They had had the typical two-minute conversation "Hi, how are you?" "How are your kids?" "Everything is great." They both admitted that they had left that encounter feeling like the other one was a wonderful mom and had a perfect family. They envied each other and what they had each *perceived* about the other's life.

Now, fast forward a few years and they are both walking into a Hurting Moms group because, in reality, they both had kids that were on drugs and living destructive lifestyles. They both had breaking hearts but they had no idea because, of course, we don't share that stuff during a chance meeting in a grocery store after many years of not seeing one another. And I'm not saying that a chance brief meeting is the appropriate place to have that conversation. I am simply making the point that our perceptions are often wrong and it is our perceptions that make us feel like we are the only mom hurting. Perhaps we can open our minds to the possibility that we are not alone. In fact, there are a whole lot of us!

Brenda said that she learned from that experience that we are as sick as our secrets, but there is healing and freedom in truth and being able to open up to others going through the same thing. Ironically, both Brenda and her friend went on to lead Hurting Moms groups.

Brenda says that if someone had told her all of those years

ago that what she was going through with her son would end up being a blessing she would have said, "yeah, right." But today she says she sees the blessing because through it, God changed her life in such an incredible way. She says that it was through reading Scripture, praying, and being surrounded by other women who were dealing with their own hurt with their children, that she found a safe place to share, cry and slowly understand that she was not alone. It drew her closer to God and she learned how to trust Him with her child. Today, she loves every opportunity to let other Hurting Moms know that they are not alone and she considers it an honor and a blessing to be able to share her story.

If your heart is breaking and you feel isolated and alone, please consider sharing your story with someone else, or join a Hurting Moms group at www.hurtingmomsmending hearts.org. You might be surprised to hear that they have experienced some of the same things. It takes courage to step out and share your most private pain, but God will give you the courage and strength that you need because He never intends for us to suffer alone. He created us to do life —including the good, the bad and the ugly—in community. We need each other. I speak from personal experience when I say, "Trust me, Mom, you are not alone! I, for one, am right here with you."

Chapter 9

Misbelief—It's My Fault

Something that Hurting Moms may not talk about, but we all certainly feel, is that we have totally failed as a parent.

We feel as though it is our fault that our son or daughter is doing what they are doing. And in some cases, we may have played a part in that. I have realized that some of my daughter's issues were a direct result of some of my behaviors while she was growing up. I divorced her abusive, alcoholic dad when she was nine and moved right in with another man who was an alcoholic. I lived with him and drank with him for six years while my kids were at critical ages. I was so wrapped up in my relationship and my alcoholism that I basically neglected my children. I had a part in my daughter's acting out and I used to be haunted by what had happened that caused such heartache. I spent a lot of time dwelling on the past, reliving periods of time and events over and over again, looking for all the ways I had gone wrong. I had a lot of "what ifs" going through my head, but there wasn't a thing I could do about any of it.

Guilt is the emotion that comes up when we feel that we are somehow at fault in what is happening with our child. Guilt is a feeling of responsibility or regret for a wrong or an offense. We experience guilt as a result of our actions, whether real or imagined. Guilt often leads to avoidance and can create dread, causing us to place responsibility for what has happened on someone else. I tried to place the blame on my daughter's father whom I had divorced. Yes, he was abusive and an alcoholic, but what about my own alcoholism? What about the fact that I moved a man, to whom I was not married, into our home? I carried a lot of guilt for many years.

I have a friend named Rachel who raised three boys as a single mom. She shared with me that for years she felt guilty because she was single and her boys were raised without their father in the home. She felt that somehow it was her fault they were spinning out of control. It was in a Hurting Moms support group that, for the first time, she could share her pain in a safe place with other moms who understood exactly what she was talking about. As Rachel worked through the ten-week curriculum, she recognized that she had done the best she could with what she had and began to experience freedom from her guilt and shame.

One of the Hurting Moms in her group reassured her that she should let go of the guilt and shame because she herself had been happily married to her husband, had raised their boys together in what she felt was a happy, stable home, and her sons had still become addicts. Whether we are single or married, our kids can become addicted, defiant, or estranged from our families. Hurting Moms come with a variety of situations, but the pain, the guilt and the shame are the same.

Maybe you can think of times that you blew it or made decisions that may have had a negative impact on your child. The first step in moving past the guilt is to face those things that we feel guilty about. Don't ignore them. Face them, admit them, and then let go of them. After all, you can't take back the things you have done in the past, but if you don't face them, they can continue their negative impact you and those you love. The truth is that, just like my friend Rachel, we all do the best we can with what we have.

I want to acknowledge here, that you may not have made choices along the way that have hurt your child. Maybe you raised your child in a loving Christian home and as you think back, there is no apparent reason from their childhood that they are acting out at this point in their lives. Remember, they are individuals, capable of making their own decisions—whether good or bad. Just because we are the mom doesn't mean we are in control or responsible for every choice our child makes. Just because our child is doing whatever it is that they are doing doesn't mean that it is our fault.

Nowhere in Scripture does it say that if we had just done the right thing as parents our child would be walking with God today. In fact, the Scriptures teach us that each person has a sinful nature and a free will. In Romans 3:24 it says, "For all have sinned and fall short of the glory of God." It says ALL, not some, but ALL have sinned.

Whether we have made mistakes as parents or not, the truth is that there is no way any of us can take back even one moment of the past. Yet I think it's safe to say that we have all longed to be released from the guilt that weighs so heavily upon us. Guilt can crush us and sap the joy out of life, leaving us lonely, bitter, and discouraged.

You may have a child who likes to remind you of the ways in which you failed him or her in the past. They are angry and bitter; they are not ready to accept responsibility for their own actions. They appear to take advantage of every opportunity to hurt you with their words. You can make a choice to let their words add to your guilt, or to move beyond the oppressive guilt that you feel by using both reason and faith to experience the joy of being forgiven and loved by God.

Once we can accept God's forgiveness and learn to forgive ourselves we can say to our child,

"That was then and this is now. I cannot go back and change the past, but I can be the best mom I know how to be to you today.

I refuse to take responsibility for the choices you are making in your life today."

There is complete freedom in not only being able to say those words, but to actually believe them!

We did the best we knew how to do and if we wronged our child, as most of us have somewhere along the way, we need to respond to the conviction of God's Spirit and experience His grace.

How have you experienced God's grace on your journey as a Hurting Mom? I began to realize that God's grace was actually evident all throughout the years of struggle with my daughter. It took a while before I started noticing, but He revealed to me that he was protecting her and answering my prayers even during some of the darkest times.

I remember one time in particular. My daughter had moved out of my house and into the house of an abusive boyfriend. She was not yet eighteen years old and I was terrified for her, but I didn't have the strength to fight her any more. Wanting to keep a door open between us I would periodically send her a card or letter just letting her know I loved her and when she was ready to come home she could.

One afternoon my stepson, her half-brother, who I didn't see very often, happened to stop by my house and he casually mentioned that he was going to something called a rave in San Bernardino that evening. I didn't think too much about it, but that night I got a call from my daughter. It was the first time I had heard her voice in several months and she was calling from a pay phone. She was scared because she and her boyfriend had gone to the rave in San Bernardino and he had abandoned her there among over 100,000 people. Now I wasn't going to drive to San Bernardino and get mixed up in this so-called rave, but I suddenly remembered my conversation with my stepson from that afternoon. I got him on the other line and was able to get the two of them together.

I'll never forget the relief I felt when he called me back to tell me they were together. She didn't come home for another couple of months, but looking back now, I know God answered my daily prayer of "Please keep her safe". That was what I prayed for every day—for her safety and for my peace. God is faithful and He does answer our prayers. I don't think it was a coincidence that my stepson stopped by out of the blue that afternoon. I believe that the cards and letters I had sent my daughter gave her the courage to reach out to me when she was frightened. It was like it had all been orchestrated by someone who could see it all and knew way ahead of time how important each of those pieces would be. Remember, even when you can't see what your child is doing, God can.

Hand in hand with guilt is another emotion that we experience which leads us to believe that what is happening is our fault. That emotion is *shame*. Shame arises as we become aware of our guilt, but it is not the same thing as guilt. Shame is that painful feeling concerning how we appear to others and it doesn't always mean that we have done something wrong. Where guilt can happen as a result of offending or hurting someone else, shame is more an inward reflection of ourselves and manifests itself with painful feelings of embarrassment and disgrace. We feel that we are the only ones who are struggling with a child who is out of control and we want to hide because we are ashamed.

I vividly remember a time when I was out to dinner with a group of women from my church. As the conversation began, they started talking about their wonderful kids. I literally wanted to get up from the table, go to my car, and drive away. I was terrified that they would turn their attention to me and ask me about my daughter.

Of course I had another daughter who was doing great, excelling in school and sports, but I could only think about the one who was using drugs and had just quit school. Isn't that typical? I was so aware of the negative things my one daughter was doing that I lost sight of the positive things my other daughter was doing. Now that was something to feel guilty about. Everything revolved around my pain and my shame at having a daughter who was out of control. I was just so sure they could see it when they looked at me and I wanted to hide.

Shame tells us that we are underserving of anything good and it discourages us and takes away our desire or motivation to change.

Here's the good news! Through Jesus we no longer have to live in guilt or shame! God wants to come close and share in our pain. We need to accept His forgiveness for any wrongdoing on our part and then learn to forgive ourselves. He knows our hearts and our minds and He empathizes with us over our children, who are also His children. We must allow His presence to reassure us and strengthen us. While God is prepared to support us in our pain, He does not intend for us to remain locked in it indefinitely. He has something better for us. But first we need to face our guilt and shame head on and deal with the deep feelings we have buried.

In the Hurting Moms Support Group that is what we do and as we face our guilt and shame, we begin to move beyond those negative emotions to experience the joy of being forgiven and loved by God. I have learned through His Word that All have sinned and fall short of the glory of God. He has taught me that I don't have to continue to own and identify with my guilt and shame.

In Romans 10:11 it says, "Anyone who believes in Him will never be put to shame." And in Psalm 34:5 it says, "Those who look to Him are radiant; their faces are never covered with shame." These verses tell me that if I trust Him and look to Him for forgiveness, peace, comfort, and joy, I do not have to live in shame.

When we begin to focus on God's opinion of us instead of our fears about the opinions of others, we become convicted. Conviction tells us when our behavior is wrong and it produces action without the feelings of worthlessness that guilt and shame cause us to feel. Conviction leads us to repentance, forgiveness, and refreshment, so we no longer feel compelled to blame anyone else.

As we examine our guilt and shame, we begin to be convicted about our actions or attitudes that may have contributed to the problems with our child. The conviction we are experiencing gives us the courage to approach those we have hurt, to restore the relationship. We put aside the pain that has been caused to us, and focus on making amends for the hurt or damage we may have caused. Once we face and acknowledge our part, we begin to experience the beginning of freedom.

I love Philippians 2: 3-4 that says, "Do nothing out of selfish ambition or vain conceit. Rather, in humility value others above yourself, not looking to your own interests but each of you to the interests of the others."

I spent quite a few years being so caught up in my own pain and heartache that I didn't really think about anyone else around me. It was all about how my daughter was making me feel. The anxiety that I woke up with every morning and the fear I carried in my heart all day, every day, about what she was doing consumed me and I became very selfish. I was so focused on my own pain that I overlooked the needs of my other kids and my husband. As I began to seek God for comfort and to learn His will, He convicted me and I knew I needed to make amends to the other people around me, people who I loved, but had neglected because I was so focused on my own heartache and my own selfishness.

As I read Scripture and sought counsel from women who were spiritually more mature than I was, I began to understand God's heart for me and for my daughter. I began to see myself the way He sees me and more importantly, I began to believe that I could be forgiven for any part I had played in our situation. God convicted me of my part and showed me that the only way I would begin to feel better was to stop focusing on my daughter and on how I was feeling and place my focus on Him and His goodness.

I clearly remember sitting at my dining room table one evening with a journal and pen and I began writing a gratitude list. Once I started writing I filled several pages of all the things I had to be grateful for. I was amazed at how good I felt when I got done and I realized that it had been a long time since I had thought about anything positive because I was so caught up in thinking about the negative, the *what ifs*, and the pain I was in.

In that moment, at my dining room table, I became convicted about the things I had done to contribute to the actions of my child, but I was also convicted about the self-centered way I had been living as I wallowed in my heartache, my guilt, and my shame.

Once I became convicted, I was eager to discover the peace that comes with knowing that God had forgiven me and I wanted to learn to forgive myself. Over time I learned to surrender my daughter and my pain to the Lord, and He began to free me from the guilt and shame I had carried for so long. There were times I had to surrender it all to him every five minutes because I was so quick to take it back, but I was consistent and God was faithful. Before long I was able to get through an entire day without feeling the incredible weight of being a Hurting Mom. He wants to free us from those negative, crippling emotions, but first we have to repent.

Repentance means to turn away from sin and turn toward God. Once we have honestly and sincerely confessed our sin and have turned away from it or repented, we will finally start to experience the peace and the joy we have longed for. God is amazingly patient with us when we are honest with Him.

Jesus paid the price for our sins when he died on the cross. Acts 13:38 says, "Therefore, my friends, I want you to know that through Jesus the forgiveness of sins is proclaimed to you." When we repent of our sins and accept the work of Jesus on the cross we can live in complete freedom from guilt and shame. Once we have been convicted and then repented, it's all out there on the table. We don't have anything to hide anymore. By repenting, we get rid of the excess baggage that continually weighs us down, and we can move on to see our lives be used by God to make a positive spiritual impact on our children. Our identity is in Jesus Christ, not in what our kids are doing and not in our own sin, which we all have, by the way. We are valued and loved by God and it is time for us to begin to value and love ourselves.

I want to encourage you to write a gratitude list today. Think about the good things in your life for which you are thankful. Thank God for His provision. Then, think about your journey as a Hurting Mom and try to identify the times God showed up and answered your prayers. How has He shown you that He is with your child? What are some specific things that have happened that have helped you to know that He hears you when you pray?

There was another time that I knew without a shadow of a doubt that God was with my daughter and with me. He answered my prayer and protected my daughter in a way that was undeniable.

She was about twenty years old and had gone to Las Vegas to work – she was a dancer in the adult entertainment industry. She was on drugs and often suffered with depression. My phone rang one night around midnight and I heard her sad, tired, lonely voice saying, "Mom, I'm in Las Vegas and

I'm so depressed. I don't think I want to live any more. I'm in my hotel room because I just couldn't bring myself to work tonight."

My heart stopped in my chest for a split second as I pleaded with God for the right words. What came out of my mouth surprised me. I said, "You are in Las Vegas and I am 250 miles away. There is nothing I can do. We are going to hang up now and you need to call a suicide hotline. I love you and I'll talk to you tomorrow."

When we hung up I tried to wake up my husband to pray with me, but he was fast asleep and I couldn't rouse him. So, I got down on my hands and knees and prayed. I asked God to comfort her and give her a sense of peace to help her fall asleep. I asked for peace for myself and then climbed back into my bed where I fell right back to sleep and slept all night.

The next morning I was at my office when she called me. The first words out of her mouth were, "Mom, did you pray for me last night?" I said, "Yes, I did—on my hands and knees." She replied, "I thought so, because as soon as we hung up I felt the sadness leave my body and a sense of peace came over me that I've never felt before. I went to sleep and slept all night long."

I remember my eyes welling up with tears because I knew God was showing me that He had her in the palm of His hand. He was faithful so many times to show me His love and my faith has grown deeper and deeper over the years. Today I totally trust Him with everything in my life, including my daughter and I never get tired of experiencing His great love for me.

As I have embraced His love I have been able to move away from the feelings of guilt and shame I had carried for so long. My identity is no longer as a Hurting Mom, but it is as a loved and blessed child of God.

Chapter 10

Misbelief—I Can Fix and Control My Child

As parents, many of us believe that we have or should have, power or control over our children. We see our child as someone we are to shape and conform into who we think they should be. In our minds, our desires, ideas and viewpoints are what matter most in life so we try to implant these in our children. This is true, and actually works, when they are little and totally dependent on us. The problem comes when we carry that over onto our teen and adult children. We feel they should still answer to us and it is hard to let go after all the years of comforting, supporting, and directing them in the way that we believed they should be raised.

Whether our child is still in our home or out on their own, we often feel that they should be obligated to us and thankful for all we have done for them over the years. We are disappointed and hurt when this doesn't happen.

Many of us thought, or assumed, that our family would always have a strong bond and it is difficult to understand that our children need to be able to find their own way of living. Unfortunately, sometimes finding their own way means that they live in ways that are contrary to what we tried to teach them, and are actually dangerous and even destructive. It's painful to just stand by and watch it happen.

It seems that overnight things change and our child is not responding to us the way they used to. I know for me, it took a long time to wake up and realize that my daughter was not going to submit to my rules. It didn't matter what I told her to do or not do—she did not respect anything I said and I had to face the fact that she was out of control – at least out of my control.

At first I thought I was just dealing with "normal" teenage stuff. And then one day it hit me over the head . . . this wasn't "normal" stuff. This was drugs and deep-rooted defiance. My daughter did not care one bit about consequences, either the ones I tried to carry out, or even consequences that went beyond me to school authorities, and even the police.

One of the first ways that I responded to my daughter was doing everything I could to control her. I would literally get into bed with her at night and try to hold her there so she wouldn't leave in the night – which was a common occurrence. I threatened, yelled and cried. She didn't care.

I took her to school every day to make sure she made it there, but she would leave once I drove away. She refused to do her school work so I wrote entire reports for her in hopes that she would just get through high school. Talk about trying to fix things! Today I wonder, "What in the world was I thinking?" I was desperate and I wasn't thinking rationally.

When trying to control her didn't work, I would often respond to her by rejecting her. It was something I did to try to make myself feel better or to mask the pain that I was experiencing because of her actions. It made me feel like I had control of something even in the midst of the chaos.

One of the ways I rejected her was to dismiss her or eliminate her from my life by kicking her out of my home. I basically let her know that as long as she was doing what she was doing I didn't want anything to do with her or have any relationship with her. I know now, that wasn't the best response. I did it in a moment of anger, which is never the time to make such an important decision.

Although there are times that having your child move out of your home can be part of setting healthy boundaries, and we did successfully employ that boundary eventually, forcing them to leave in the moment of anger or rage, is a severe form of rejection and narrows the chance for eventual reconciliation because the child feels that they are no longer part of the family.

Another form of rejection, which is much more subtle and definitely less direct, is to ignore or refuse to consider our child. I tried this as well and, although rejecting her in this way was more passive, it caused a tremendous amount of tension in our home and it sometimes dragged on for weeks or months at a time which affected our entire family in a negative way. Rejecting her in this way did not help us to move in the direction of resolving any of the issues that were causing the problems or the distance between us.

There finally came a point where I realized I had to let her go. The anguish and feeling of futility I was experiencing from trying to control—what was out of my control—was killing me inside.

Why is it that we keep trying to hold on? There are so many reasons, aren't there? For one thing, being a mom is such a huge part of who we are that releasing our children may seem impossible. This loss feels like the end of life as we have known it. Yet the reality is, that it is a new chapter in our lives. It does change the dynamic in our home and in our relationship with our child.

We often try to hold on because we feel like we have completely blown it as a parent and if we let go we will be admitting that our efforts at trying to fix or control them have not worked and even worse, that we have failed as parents.

Another reason we try to hold on to our kids is that we are afraid that once we let go we will be unable to shield or safeguard them from harm. But let's face it, the harm is being caused by their own choices and although we have tried, there is nothing we can really do about it. However, that doesn't stop us from trying, does it? We run ourselves in circles trying to protect our kids from having to pay the consequences of their choices. And, in fact, we are the ones that often get in the way and prevent them from getting to the end of themselves, and even worse, we get in the way of what God might be trying to do in them.

I have known many parents who continue to enable their drug addicted or alcoholic kids even after they have been lied to, stolen from, and verbally, as well as sometimes physically, abused. They are held hostage in their own homes and yet still, they cannot bring themselves to allow their child to pay the consequences for their actions.

I love the story of the Prodigal Son found in the 15th chapter of Luke. The father in this story is a wonderful example of a parent who "let go" of his child. This dad loved his son and he knew his boy would make bad choices when he left home, yet the dad didn't try to control his son by refusing to give him his inheritance. He certainly could have controlled at least that aspect of what was happening. But he didn't. He gave his son his inheritance and allowed him to go and to make his own mistakes. Letting him go and allowing him to squander all of his money so that he ended up eating with the pigs was exactly what that young man needed to realize that what he had had wasn't so bad after all. He went home and asked his father for forgiveness. That would never have happened if that dad had not let go of his son.

What does surrendering our child mean? How do we do it?

Remember, surrendering does not mean that we give up on our child, but it does mean that we stop trying to fix and control them. If we give up on someone, we abandon them. Surrendering means that we let go and give our child the freedom to make mistakes, but we also allow them to pay the consequences for those mistakes.

Surrendering our children means that we trust God more and we rely less on what our child is doing or not doing for our sense of well-being. It means we become free from the emotional roller coaster ride because our emotional state is no longer reliant on our child's actions. Surrendering our child means that we give them the independence they need so they can be motivated by God instead of by our nagging, meddling, or manipulation.

When we surrender our child we begin to see that we are not responsible for the choices they are making, which reduces the guilt we have been experiencing.

Letting go of my daughter did not mean that I turned my back on her or that I didn't love her any more—it meant surrendering her to God and allowing Him to be the one to work in her life. Trust me when I tell you that this didn't happen overnight. It was a process. There were days when I was successful at trusting God with her and then there were other days where I would find myself right back in the middle of her mess. There are still times with all my kids (who are all grown) that I have to re-surrender them to Him because I find myself getting caught up in their stuff again. The difference now is that I have the tools I need to be able to do that.

Being a mom is such a huge part of who we are that releasing our children seems impossible. It feels like such a huge loss. Even though my efforts at trying to fix my daughter did not work, I felt that if I let go of her I was admitting failure as her mom. It meant that I had to stop trying to protect her from harm. The reality was that the harm was being caused by her own choices that I had no control over so there was no way I could protect her anyway.

There are several unhealthy ways that we try to hold on to or control our children. Even though we have good intentions —they can actually be detrimental to our child and to ourselves.

We Sacrifice: It is so easy to lose ourselves by constantly putting our child first. When they are young this is what we do, right? Moms sacrifice! It just goes with the job. The problem is that when they grow up and we continue to put ourselves out there to protect them from paying the consequences of their actions we are not helping them. In fact, we are slowing down their development and keeping them out of reality. And in the meanwhile, we exhaust ourselves and ruin our other relationships because we are so busy giving everything we have to our child.

We see ourselves as their Savior: We cannot save or protect them! We often feel guilty if we know our child needs help and refuses to get it for themselves. We feel that it is our responsibility to make them better. But again, our actions or attitudes can be the very things that get in the way of something God is trying to do in the life of our child. *He* is the Savior . . . we are not!

We are Selfish: We often lose sight of what is really going on with our child because we become so caught up in how we are feeling because of their actions. We want to regulate them by trying to make them feel guilty about not being thankful for all we have done for them. We are afraid that if we separate ourselves from our child we won't be needed any longer. We get so wrapped up in our pain and in trying to control our child that it starts to be all about us. Our identity becomes about being a Hurting Mom, we are the victim, and we forget who we really are apart from that identity.

One of the most powerful aspects of being in a Hurting Moms group is that we learn to surrender our children to the God who created them and loves them more that we do. We learn to let go, which by the way, doesn't mean we don't love them or have a relationship with them. It simply means we let them pay the consequences for their own decisions and refuse to allow them to control our lives.

We never separate from our child, but we disengage ourselves from their problematic behavior. We are able to do this as we realize that our child is a distinct and detached being. If we are to overcome the negative emotions that have been destroying us, we have to begin to disengage from our child and allow them to begin to develop their own individuality.

Surrendering our child, disengaging from our child, letting go of our child, these are all choices on our part. It isn't easy, and it won't happen by itself. We have to make a deliberate decision to do it. Remember, relinquishment is giving someone up, but abandonment is giving up on someone.

We are **NOT** abandoning our kids by disengaging from them, surrendering them, or letting them go. Remember that letter I wrote to Leah when she had left with her abusive boyfriend? That was my way of keeping the door open for her to come home, but on my terms. I wanted her to know that when she was ready to come back to her family, we would welcome her back with open arms. I had disengaged from her, but I made sure that she knew I had not abandoned her.

The belief that if we just keep trying to fix or control them, our children will eventually get it and turn around is another misbelief! If our child is going to turn around, it is not going to be because of anything we do, it's going to be because we get out of the way and let God do what He wants to do.

Chapter 11

Misbelief—I'll Never Have Peace or Joy

Have you ever tried to find a birthday card, Christmas card or a Valentine for the child who is causing you pain? If you are anything like me, it probably wasn't a very good experience. I remember standing in front of the cards for "daughters" feeling overwhelmed because I couldn't find a card that expressed how I felt about mine. They all had catchy, upbeat phrases that sang the praises of the recipient, but I wasn't feeling proud of my daughter and she certainly wasn't bringing me any joy. I loved my daughter, but I really didn't like her in those days. I would read a card and put it back, read another card and put it back, until I had read every card on the rack.

Most of the time I would just end up buying a benign card that didn't even mention the word "daughter". I often wondered why I was even bothering to look for a card for her in the first place, then I would remember that this was *my* child, the baby I had held in my arms with so much hope and anticipation for her future. And my heart would break all over again. Something as simple as buying a card could absolutely steal my joy and my peace right out from under me.

For so long our joy, peace, and basic sense of well-being have been wrapped up in our children. If they are ok, we are ok. But, if they get caught up in lifestyles or habits that are contrary to what we know to be the right way to live—we have a difficult time focusing on anything else. Especially if what they are doing is dangerous or destructive. We can't seem to function because we are so frightened for their safety. Sleep eludes us when we get into bed at night and we wake up in the morning with a gnawing ache in our very core. We don't think we can move beyond the pain and emptiness we are experiencing, and feelings of hopelessness threaten to consume us. Even when we are with our friends or other family members for what should be happy or joyous occasions we continue to experience that constant and painful nagging feeling of unrest.

Although we can't control the actions of our child, the one thing we can control is how we react to them. We may try to mask our pain by using alcohol or drugs. For some of us, the way we react or cope with the situation is to shop, or eat, or work, or sleep. Regardless of what we do to try to medicate or numb ourselves from the pain, we still cannot find the peace and joy that we are seeking. Scripture shows us that our reactions to our child's behavior can cause us to feel separated from God, who is the only true source of peace. In Psalm 68:19 it says,

"Praise be to the Lord, to God our Savior, who daily bears our burdens." And in Matthew 11:28 Jesus said, "Come to me, all you who are weary and burdened and I will give you rest."

These Scriptures give us the answer to our heartache but we must let go of the baggage of our negative reactions. God can't carry our burdens if we don't hand them over to him. Of course, that is easier said than done! The Scriptures also say, "I can do all things through Him who gives me strength." In other words, the things that seem too hard or even impossible for us to do alone, are totally doable if we will just tap into the strength of Jesus and allow Him to give us the rest we need.

Let's examine some of the emotions and attitudes that get in the way of our joy and peace. These are the negative emotions that we just keep holding onto even though they are hurting us and keeping us from enjoying the peace that God is waiting to give us.

First of all, I think it's safe to say that when we have a wayward child we experience a deep sense of disappointment. Disappointment produces negative feelings and attitudes that lead to sadness and even depression. It digs deeply into our sense of contentment and well-being. If our hope is based on what our child is doing, we are going to be disappointed. In fact, if we place our hope in any human we will probably be disappointed. However, if we place our hope in the Lord, we will experience just the opposite. In Isaiah 49:23b it says, "…Then you will know that I am the Lord; those who hope in me will not be disappointed."

We hope that our child will turn around. We pray that God will fix them and we even try to fix them ourselves. There is no peace in that—it just leads to disappointment. I often talk to moms who tell me about all the ways they have tried to fix or control their child and I always ask them the same question, "How has trying to fix or control your child worked out so far?" The answer is always the same, "It hasn't worked out well at all." When we try repeatedly to fix our kids, we are left with a bitter sense of disappointment and the fear and anxiety continue to tear us up inside. It isn't until we move away from placing our hope in the changes that may or may not happen in our child and put our hope in the Lord that we can and will begin to have peace, even in the midst of the struggle.

Another emotion that gets in the way of our peace and joy is anger. Anger may at first be a natural and healthy response to our pain. But if it is not dealt with and resolved, it can burrow in and take up permanent residence. My anger towards my daughter ran deep. I was so resentful of her because I felt that she was ruining my life. I wasn't able function as the mom or wife that I wanted to be with the rest of my family nor enjoy time with them because I was so consumed with negative feelings and especially anger toward her. I took days and even weeks at a time off from work to deal with her and was furious that I had to take parenting classes because she was continuously truant from school. She created chaos and instability in our home and I was frustrated, angry, and bitter. Of course the anger rotated with feelings of sadness and fear. But it was always there, just below the surface.

It was out of desperation that I began to seek God in the midst of my trial. I spent time reading my Bible and praying and I sought out wisdom from Christian women who were more mature than I was. I focused on looking up Scripture that talked about anger and as I read from His Word I began to see God's heart for me and it became very clear that He did not want me to be angry. In the first chapter of the book of James it says, "Everyone should be quick to listen, slow to speak and *slow to become angry*, for man's anger does not bring about the righteous life that God desires." And in Ephesians 4:26 is says, "In your anger do not sin; do not let the sun go down while you are still angry."

My first reaction was to say, "Oh yeah, God, it's easy for you to say, 'don't be angry'. I don't have any control over my anger." But as I continued to go deeper in my relationship with Him, I realized that He wasn't just telling me not to be angry. He was telling me that He wanted to help me to overcome my anger. He knows that we are powerless over our emotions and alone we are unable to control them. Releasing our anger and allowing God to comfort us is not easy, but it is possible if we will surrender it to the God who loves us and doesn't want us to continue in our suffering. At first it is a moment by moment process. It means stopping and making a conscious decision to let it go whenever we feel it coming over us. Eventually, the angry spells become fewer and farther between.

Hurt is another negative emotion that we feel when our child is going down a path of destruction. They have turned their backs on everything that we value and have tried to instill in them. It is painful! We usually associate the word hurt with physical pain, but we can be left reeling emotionally when we are hit where we are most vulnerable—in our hearts. The pain we feel is overwhelming sometimes and we don't know how to move beyond it. We have a God who loves us so much that when we hurt, He hurts with us. Somehow, it is comforting to know that we are not alone in it.

Fear and anxiety stem from the fact that we are often afraid for the safety of our child. We worry about what will happen to them if they continue down the road they are on and we feel anxious about where they are and what they are doing. What bad decision will our child make to hurt themselves or others? How can we protect them? The bottom line is that we cannot protect our kids from their bad choices. In fact, we need to let them pay the consequences for their own decisions. I think that we are the ones who often get in the way of what God is trying to do in their lives. We protect them and cover for them, and they never have to deal with the results of their bad choices.

I remember writing entire reports for my daughter because she was pretty much flunking out of high school. I can tell you that my intervening in her schoolwork did absolutely nothing to help. She still didn't graduate from high school! I will say that I know more today about Queen Elizabeth and cockatiels than I ever did before—thanks to my report writing for her. I was so terrified that if she didn't graduate from high school, my life would be ruined. Once it became apparent that she was not going to finish, and I let go of it—because I had no other choice—I experienced a huge sense of relief. One of the things that I had been most afraid of and had caused me a tremendous amount of anxiety actually happened—and it didn't kill me! That's the secret to peace. We have to let go and receive the peace that Jesus wants for us to have. Why do we insist on hanging on to the very things that are hurting us?

- When we surrender our children we stop being accountable for them, but we still follow through on our obligations to them.
- When we surrender our child we trust God more and we rely less on what our child is doing or not doing for our own sense of well-being and we give them the independence they need so they can be motivated by God instead of by our nagging, meddling, or manipulation.
- When we surrender our child we become free from the emotional roller-coaster ride because our emotional state is no longer reliant on our child's actions.
- And when we surrender our child we begin to see that we are not responsible for their choices which reduces the guilt that we have been carrying around for so long.

The Bible tells us that our joy and our peace come from Christ. There is no way that anyone else can rob us of that unless we allow them to. That's where the problem lies—by holding onto them, we continue to allow our kids to prevent us from experiencing the good things that God wants to give us. We DO have a choice in this, but most of the time we choose to allow our fear, anger, and anxiety to take over instead of seeking His grace and the peace that comes with it.

I would ask God for his perfect peace, sometimes many times a day. Whenever I asked for it, I would immediately feel it pouring over me and for a few minutes, I would have relief from my anguish . . . until I turned my focus back to my child, which was often almost immediately. But, I did experience His peace EVERY time I asked for it and I knew He was listening. Sometimes, it would help to go through the physical motion of reaching up and grabbing peace and pulling it to my heart.

Try that right now. Reach up, grab the peace (close your fist around it) and pull it to your heart. DO IT AGAIN. This is something you can do when you feel that anxiety threatening to take over. It may seem kind of silly, but it works!!!

As I disciplined myself to ask God for his peace, what began to happen was that over time, I found I could hang onto His peace for longer and longer periods of time. It became a habit for me to seek Him and sense His presence throughout my day.

Another thing that really helped me was to focus on a couple of my favorite Scriptures:

In John 14:27 Jesus says, "Peace I leave with you; My peace I give you. I do not give to you as the world gives. Do not let your hearts be troubled and do not be afraid." And in Joshua 1:9 it says, "…Be strong and courageous. Do not be afraid; do not be discouraged, for the Lord your God will be with you wherever you go."

There are lots of other Scriptures that remind us that we are not alone. God cares about us and wants us to have peace, even in the middle of the storms of our lives. Reading those promises in the Bible is a powerful tool.

Along my journey as a Hurting Mom, when my daughter was making horrendous choices, God showed up to remind me He was there with me and with her. He had been there all along, but it took me awhile to realize it. I had shut myself off from everyone, including Him.

My daughter was using drugs, dancing in the adult entertainment industry, in and out of abusive relationships, had multiple abortions, and was living totally outside of God's plan for her. All of those things that she was doing—the very things that were breaking my heart—are the things that God used to bring me back to Himself. It was when I finally got to the end of myself, admitted my powerlessness in the situation and surrendered it all to Him, that I began to have relief from the agonizing pain I had been in.

I had been raised in the church and accepted Christ when I was fifteen years old, but I hadn't followed Him or been in a real relationship with Him for many years. It was out of desperation, pain, and guilt that I went back to church. It was because of my own hurt, anxiety, and fear over my daughter that I started the Hurting Moms group where I not only began to heal, but I grew closer to God. Later, when I got involved in Celebrate Recovery I began to recognize that the healing for which I had longed was already taking place in my life. By surrendering my life (including my desire to control my daughter, even though her life was still spiraling out of control) to Jesus, I began to experience real joy and peace again.

Chapter 12

Conclusion

While I was getting better by learning to rely on the Lord and to trust Him with my life and the life of my daughter, she was in a whole lot of pain and suffered with some pretty serious depression. She was still making very damaging and destructive choices for herself, but she began to see the changes in my life and she started to periodically show up at Celebrate Recovery. At first it was out of curiosity, but then, she said that her depression was lifted and she felt better when she was there—especially during the worship music. Soon she came on a regular basis and within a year or so she started coming to church on Sunday. She still had things going on that I'm sure were not part of God's plan for her, but I was grateful for the positive changes that I could see in her life and slowly over time healing began to take place in our relationship. About six years ago I had the honor and privilege of baptizing her and her then six-year-old daughter.

I have focused on my one daughter for most of this book,

but I want you to know that I have raised a total of eight kids, both biological and step, who are all adults now. We've already established that just because they grow up doesn't mean we stop being their mom, we just learn how to do it differently than we did when they were young. With as many kids as I have, there is always at least one of them who is going through something that can threaten to rob my peace and my joy. It is hard to be okay if our kids aren't okay.

When I start to get anxious about something one of my kids is doing or going through today, I simply think back to the times that God showed up when I thought there was no hope. I remember the signs that He was working behind the scenes and I still hold on to those memories today. When things aren't going well or I start to get stressed out or anxious about anything, I stop and remember the hope I have in Christ Jesus because I know He is busy at work in my life even when I can't see or sense it.

I am living proof that believing that there is no hope for peace in my life until my child turned around is a huge misbelief! I have learned to have peace and joy even in the middle of the chaos. The tools in this book and the material in the Hurting Moms groups are tools I use every day, whether I'm in a crisis or not. I love being wrapped in God's grace and all the good things that come from trusting Him and I don't want to miss out on that.

Don't get me wrong . . . there are still those times that I forget, for a little while, that I am not in control. There are those times when I start trying to interfere in the lives of my children because I think that I have the solution to their problems. But just as soon as I start down that path, I can literally feel my joy and peace being sapped right out of me, which I believe is God's reminder to let go and re-surrender it all to Him.

My prayer for all Hurting Moms today is that you will begin to let go of your desire to fix and control your child and learn to trust God with them. Allow Him to be the one to comfort you and give you the strength to let your child pay their own consequences for their choices. Stop blaming yourself for the choices of your child, and as you surrender them to the God who created them and loves them more than you do, you will to experience the joy and peace that you are longing for. Remember, you are not alone!

To find out more about a Hurting Moms, Mending Hearts support group go to @hurtingmoms Facebook page or www.Hurtingmomsmendinghearts.org. Get the help you deserve today.

WAYS TO GET CONNECTED TO
THE HM COMMUNITY

- Sign up for <u>FREE</u> Daily Encouraging Words email series at www.hurtingmomsmendinghearts.org

- Follow us on Facebook @hurtingmoms

- Watch our Facebook live show "Real Stories of Hurting Moms" - Thursdays 6 pm (Pacific Time) (FB @hurtingmoms)

- Join a HM "Breaking Free" Support Group— www.hurtingmomsmendinghearts.org/Groups

- Start a group in your area— www.hurtingmomsmendinghearts.org/leaders